GNU Diffutils Reference Manual

A catalogue record for this book is available from the Hong Kong Public Libraries.

Published in Hong Kong by Samurai Media Limited.

Email: info@samuraimedia.org

ISBN 978-988-8381-54-8

Background Cover Image by https://www.flickr.com/people/webtreatsetc/

Short Contents

Table of Contents

Overview

Computer users often find occasion to ask how two files differ. Perhaps one file is a newer version of the other file. Or maybe the two files started out as identical copies but were changed by different people.

You can use the `diff` command to show differences between two files, or each corresponding file in two directories. `diff` outputs differences between files line by line in any of several formats, selectable by command line options. This set of differences is often called a *diff* or *patch*. For files that are identical, `diff` normally produces no output; for binary (non-text) files, `diff` normally reports only that they are different.

You can use the `cmp` command to show the byte and line numbers where two files differ. `cmp` can also show all the bytes that differ between the two files, side by side. A way to compare two files character by character is the Emacs command `M-x compare-windows`. See Section "Other Window" in *The GNU Emacs Manual*, for more information on that command.

You can use the `diff3` command to show differences among three files. When two people have made independent changes to a common original, `diff3` can report the differences between the original and the two changed versions, and can produce a merged file that contains both persons' changes together with warnings about conflicts.

You can use the `sdiff` command to merge two files interactively.

You can use the set of differences produced by `diff` to distribute updates to text files (such as program source code) to other people. This method is especially useful when the differences are small compared to the complete files. Given `diff` output, you can use the `patch` program to update, or *patch*, a copy of the file. If you think of `diff` as subtracting one file from another to produce their difference, you can think of `patch` as adding the difference to one file to reproduce the other.

This manual first concentrates on making diffs, and later shows how to use diffs to update files.

GNU `diff` was written by Paul Eggert, Mike Haertel, David Hayes, Richard Stallman, and Len Tower. Wayne Davison designed and implemented the unified output format. The basic algorithm is described by Eugene W. Myers in "An O(ND) Difference Algorithm and its Variations", *Algorithmica* Vol. 1 No. 2, 1986, pp. 251–266; and in "A File Comparison Program", Webb Miller and Eugene W. Myers, *Software—Practice and Experience* Vol. 15 No. 11, 1985, pp. 1025–1040. The algorithm was independently discovered as described by E. Ukkonen in "Algorithms for Approximate String Matching", *Information and Control* Vol. 64, 1985, pp. 100–118. Unless the '`--minimal`' option is used, `diff` uses a heuristic by Paul Eggert that limits the cost to $O(N^1.5logN)$ at the price of producing suboptimal output for large inputs with many differences. Related algorithms are surveyed by Alfred V. Aho in section 6.3 of "Algorithms for Finding Patterns in Strings", *Handbook of Theoretical Computer Science* (Jan Van Leeuwen, ed.), Vol. A, *Algorithms and Complexity*, Elsevier/MIT Press, 1990, pp. 255–300.

GNU `diff3` was written by Randy Smith. GNU `sdiff` was written by Thomas Lord. GNU `cmp` was written by Torbjörn Granlund and David MacKenzie.

GNU `patch` was written mainly by Larry Wall and Paul Eggert; several GNU enhancements were contributed by Wayne Davison and David MacKenzie. Parts of this manual are adapted from a manual page written by Larry Wall, with his permission.

1 What Comparison Means

There are several ways to think about the differences between two files. One way to think of the differences is as a series of lines that were deleted from, inserted in, or changed in one file to produce the other file. `diff` compares two files line by line, finds groups of lines that differ, and reports each group of differing lines. It can report the differing lines in several formats, which have different purposes.

GNU `diff` can show whether files are different without detailing the differences. It also provides ways to suppress certain kinds of differences that are not important to you. Most commonly, such differences are changes in the amount of white space between words or lines. `diff` also provides ways to suppress differences in alphabetic case or in lines that match a regular expression that you provide. These options can accumulate; for example, you can ignore changes in both white space and alphabetic case.

Another way to think of the differences between two files is as a sequence of pairs of bytes that can be either identical or different. `cmp` reports the differences between two files byte by byte, instead of line by line. As a result, it is often more useful than `diff` for comparing binary files. For text files, `cmp` is useful mainly when you want to know only whether two files are identical, or whether one file is a prefix of the other.

To illustrate the effect that considering changes byte by byte can have compared with considering them line by line, think of what happens if a single newline character is added to the beginning of a file. If that file is then compared with an otherwise identical file that lacks the newline at the beginning, `diff` will report that a blank line has been added to the file, while `cmp` will report that almost every byte of the two files differs.

`diff3` normally compares three input files line by line, finds groups of lines that differ, and reports each group of differing lines. Its output is designed to make it easy to inspect two different sets of changes to the same file.

1.1 Hunks

When comparing two files, `diff` finds sequences of lines common to both files, interspersed with groups of differing lines called *hunks*. Comparing two identical files yields one sequence of common lines and no hunks, because no lines differ. Comparing two entirely different files yields no common lines and one large hunk that contains all lines of both files. In general, there are many ways to match up lines between two given files. `diff` tries to minimize the total hunk size by finding large sequences of common lines interspersed with small hunks of differing lines.

For example, suppose the file 'F' contains the three lines 'a', 'b', 'c', and the file 'G' contains the same three lines in reverse order 'c', 'b', 'a'. If `diff` finds the line 'c' as common, then the command 'diff F G' produces this output:

```
1,2d0
< a
< b
3a2,3
> b
> a
```

But if `diff` notices the common line 'b' instead, it produces this output:

```
1c1
< a
---
> c
3c3
< c
---
> a
```

It is also possible to find 'a' as the common line. `diff` does not always find an optimal matching between the files; it takes shortcuts to run faster. But its output is usually close to the shortest possible. You can adjust this tradeoff with the '--minimal' ('-d') option (see Chapter 6 [diff Performance], page 33).

1.2 Suppressing Differences in Blank and Tab Spacing

The '--ignore-tab-expansion' ('-E') option ignores the distinction between tabs and spaces on input. A tab is considered to be equivalent to the number of spaces to the next tab stop (see Section 5.1 [Tabs], page 31).

The '--ignore-trailing-space' ('-Z') option ignores white space at line end.

The '--ignore-space-change' ('-b') option is stronger than '-E' and '-Z' combined. It ignores white space at line end, and considers all other sequences of one or more white space characters within a line to be equivalent. With this option, `diff` considers the following two lines to be equivalent, where '$' denotes the line end:

```
Here lyeth  muche rychnesse  in lytell space.   -- John Heywood$
Here lyeth muche rychnesse in lytell space. -- John Heywood    $
```

The '--ignore-all-space' ('-w') option is stronger still. It ignores differences even if one line has white space where the other line has none. *White space* characters include tab, vertical tab, form feed, carriage return, and space; some locales may define additional characters to be white space. With this option, `diff` considers the following two lines to be equivalent, where '$' denotes the line end and '^M' denotes a carriage return:

```
Here lyeth  muche  rychnesse in lytell space.--   John Heywood$
 He relyeth much erychnes  seinly tells pace.  --John Heywood    ^M$
```

For many other programs newline is also a white space character, but `diff` is a line-oriented program and a newline character always ends a line. Hence the '-w' or '--ignore-all-space' option does not ignore newline-related changes; it ignores only other white space changes.

1.3 Suppressing Differences Whose Lines Are All Blank

The '--ignore-blank-lines' ('-B') option ignores changes that consist entirely of blank lines. With this option, for example, a file containing

```
1.  A point is that which has no part.


2.  A line is breadthless length.
-- Euclid, The Elements, I
```

is considered identical to a file containing

```
    1.  A point is that which has no part.
    2.  A line is breadthless length.


    -- Euclid, The Elements, I
```

Normally this option affects only lines that are completely empty, but if you also specify an option that ignores trailing spaces, lines are also affected if they look empty but contain white space. In other words, '-B' is equivalent to '-I '^$'' by default, but it is equivalent to '-I '^[[:space:]]*$'' if '-b', '-w' or '-Z' is also specified.

1.4 Suppressing Differences Whose Lines All Match a Regular Expression

To ignore insertions and deletions of lines that match a **grep**-style regular expression, use the '--ignore-matching-lines=*regexp*' ('-I *regexp*') option. You should escape regular expressions that contain shell metacharacters to prevent the shell from expanding them. For example, 'diff -I '^[[:digit:]]'' ignores all changes to lines beginning with a digit.

However, '-I' only ignores the insertion or deletion of lines that contain the regular expression if every changed line in the hunk—every insertion and every deletion—matches the regular expression. In other words, for each nonignorable change, **diff** prints the complete set of changes in its vicinity, including the ignorable ones.

You can specify more than one regular expression for lines to ignore by using more than one '-I' option. **diff** tries to match each line against each regular expression.

1.5 Suppressing Case Differences

GNU **diff** can treat lower case letters as equivalent to their upper case counterparts, so that, for example, it considers 'Funky Stuff', 'funky STUFF', and 'fUNKy stuFf' to all be the same. To request this, use the '-i' or '--ignore-case' option.

1.6 Summarizing Which Files Differ

When you only want to find out whether files are different, and you don't care what the differences are, you can use the summary output format. In this format, instead of showing the differences between the files, **diff** simply reports whether files differ. The '--brief' ('-q') option selects this output format.

This format is especially useful when comparing the contents of two directories. It is also much faster than doing the normal line by line comparisons, because **diff** can stop analyzing the files as soon as it knows that there are any differences.

You can also get a brief indication of whether two files differ by using **cmp**. For files that are identical, **cmp** produces no output. When the files differ, by default, **cmp** outputs the byte and line number where the first difference occurs, or reports that one file is a prefix of the other. You can use the '-s', '--quiet', or '--silent' option to suppress that information, so that **cmp** produces no output and reports whether the files differ using only its exit status (see Chapter 12 [Invoking cmp], page 57).

Unlike **diff**, **cmp** cannot compare directories; it can only compare two files.

1.7 Binary Files and Forcing Text Comparisons

If `diff` thinks that either of the two files it is comparing is binary (a non-text file), it normally treats that pair of files much as if the summary output format had been selected (see Section 1.6 [Brief], page 5), and reports only that the binary files are different. This is because line by line comparisons are usually not meaningful for binary files.

`diff` determines whether a file is text or binary by checking the first few bytes in the file; the exact number of bytes is system dependent, but it is typically several thousand. If every byte in that part of the file is non-null, `diff` considers the file to be text; otherwise it considers the file to be binary.

Sometimes you might want to force `diff` to consider files to be text. For example, you might be comparing text files that contain null characters; `diff` would erroneously decide that those are non-text files. Or you might be comparing documents that are in a format used by a word processing system that uses null characters to indicate special formatting. You can force `diff` to consider all files to be text files, and compare them line by line, by using the '`--text`' ('`-a`') option. If the files you compare using this option do not in fact contain text, they will probably contain few newline characters, and the `diff` output will consist of hunks showing differences between long lines of whatever characters the files contain.

You can also force `diff` to report only whether files differ (but not how). Use the '`--brief`' ('`-q`') option for this.

Normally, differing binary files count as trouble because the resulting `diff` output does not capture all the differences. This trouble causes `diff` to exit with status 2. However, this trouble cannot occur with the '`--text`' ('`-a`') option, or with the '`--brief`' ('`-q`') option, as these options both cause `diff` to generate a form of output that represents differences as requested.

In operating systems that distinguish between text and binary files, `diff` normally reads and writes all data as text. Use the '`--binary`' option to force `diff` to read and write binary data instead. This option has no effect on a POSIX-compliant system like GNU or traditional Unix. However, many personal computer operating systems represent the end of a line with a carriage return followed by a newline. On such systems, `diff` normally ignores these carriage returns on input and generates them at the end of each output line, but with the '`--binary`' option `diff` treats each carriage return as just another input character, and does not generate a carriage return at the end of each output line. This can be useful when dealing with non-text files that are meant to be interchanged with POSIX-compliant systems.

The '`--strip-trailing-cr`' causes `diff` to treat input lines that end in carriage return followed by newline as if they end in plain newline. This can be useful when comparing text that is imperfectly imported from many personal computer operating systems. This option affects how lines are read, which in turn affects how they are compared and output.

If you want to compare two files byte by byte, you can use the `cmp` program with the '`--verbose`' ('`-l`') option to show the values of each differing byte in the two files. With GNU `cmp`, you can also use the '`-b`' or '`--print-bytes`' option to show the ASCII representation of those bytes. See Chapter 12 [Invoking cmp], page 57, for more information.

If `diff3` thinks that any of the files it is comparing is binary (a non-text file), it normally reports an error, because such comparisons are usually not useful. `diff3` uses the same test as `diff` to decide whether a file is binary. As with `diff`, if the input files contain a few non-text bytes but otherwise are like text files, you can force `diff3` to consider all files to be text files and compare them line by line by using the '`-a`' or '`--text`' option.

2 `diff` Output Formats

`diff` has several mutually exclusive options for output format. The following sections describe each format, illustrating how `diff` reports the differences between two sample input files.

2.1 Two Sample Input Files

Here are two sample files that we will use in numerous examples to illustrate the output of `diff` and how various options can change it.

This is the file 'lao':

```
The Way that can be told of is not the eternal Way;
The name that can be named is not the eternal name.
The Nameless is the origin of Heaven and Earth;
The Named is the mother of all things.
Therefore let there always be non-being,
  so we may see their subtlety,
And let there always be being,
  so we may see their outcome.
The two are the same,
But after they are produced,
  they have different names.
```

This is the file 'tzu':

```
The Nameless is the origin of Heaven and Earth;
The named is the mother of all things.

Therefore let there always be non-being,
  so we may see their subtlety,
And let there always be being,
  so we may see their outcome.
The two are the same,
But after they are produced,
  they have different names.
They both may be called deep and profound.
Deeper and more profound,
The door of all subtleties!
```

In this example, the first hunk contains just the first two lines of 'lao', the second hunk contains the fourth line of 'lao' opposing the second and third lines of 'tzu', and the last hunk contains just the last three lines of 'tzu'.

2.2 Showing Differences in Their Context

Usually, when you are looking at the differences between files, you will also want to see the parts of the files near the lines that differ, to help you understand exactly what has changed. These nearby parts of the files are called the *context*.

GNU `diff` provides two output formats that show context around the differing lines: *context format* and *unified format*. It can optionally show in which function or section of the file the differing lines are found.

If you are distributing new versions of files to other people in the form of `diff` output, you should use one of the output formats that show context so that they can apply the diffs even if they have made small changes of their own to the files. `patch` can apply the diffs in this case by searching in the files for the lines of context around the differing lines; if those lines are actually a few lines away from where the diff says they are, `patch` can adjust the line numbers accordingly and still apply the diff correctly. See Section 10.3 [Imperfect], page 46, for more information on using `patch` to apply imperfect diffs.

2.2.1 Context Format

The context output format shows several lines of context around the lines that differ. It is the standard format for distributing updates to source code.

To select this output format, use the '`--context[=lines]`' ('`-C lines`') or '`-c`' option. The argument *lines* that some of these options take is the number of lines of context to show. If you do not specify *lines*, it defaults to three. For proper operation, `patch` typically needs at least two lines of context.

2.2.1.1 An Example of Context Format

Here is the output of '`diff -c lao tzu`' (see Section 2.1 [Sample diff Input], page 9, for the complete contents of the two files). Notice that up to three lines that are not different are shown around each line that is different; they are the context lines. Also notice that the first two hunks have run together, because their contents overlap.

```
*** lao 2002-02-21 23:30:39.942229878 -0800
--- tzu 2002-02-21 23:30:50.442260588 -0800
***************
*** 1,7 ****
- The Way that can be told of is not the eternal Way;
- The name that can be named is not the eternal name.
  The Nameless is the origin of Heaven and Earth;
! The Named is the mother of all things.
  Therefore let there always be non-being,
    so we may see their subtlety,
  And let there always be being,
--- 1,6 ----
  The Nameless is the origin of Heaven and Earth;
! The named is the mother of all things.
!
  Therefore let there always be non-being,
    so we may see their subtlety,
  And let there always be being,
***************
*** 9,11 ****
--- 8,13 ----
  The two are the same,
```

```
      But after they are produced,
         they have different names.
    + They both may be called deep and profound.
    + Deeper and more profound,
    + The door of all subtleties!
```

2.2.1.2 An Example of Context Format with Less Context

Here is the output of 'diff -C 1 lao tzu' (see Section 2.1 [Sample diff Input], page 9, for the complete contents of the two files). Notice that at most one context line is reported here.

```
*** lao 2002-02-21 23:30:39.942229878 -0800
--- tzu 2002-02-21 23:30:50.442260588 -0800
***************
*** 1,5 ****
- The Way that can be told of is not the eternal Way;
- The name that can be named is not the eternal name.
  The Nameless is the origin of Heaven and Earth;
! The Named is the mother of all things.
  Therefore let there always be non-being,
--- 1,4 ----
  The Nameless is the origin of Heaven and Earth;
! The named is the mother of all things.
!
  Therefore let there always be non-being,
***************
*** 11 ****
--- 10,13 ----
     they have different names.
  + They both may be called deep and profound.
  + Deeper and more profound,
  + The door of all subtleties!
```

2.2.1.3 Detailed Description of Context Format

The context output format starts with a two-line header, which looks like this:

```
*** from-file from-file-modification-time
--- to-file to-file-modification time
```

The time stamp normally looks like '2002-02-21 23:30:39.942229878 -0800' to indicate the date, time with fractional seconds, and time zone in Internet RFC 2822 format. (The fractional seconds are omitted on hosts that do not support fractional time stamps.) However, a traditional time stamp like 'Thu Feb 21 23:30:39 2002' is used if the LC_TIME locale category is either 'C' or 'POSIX'.

You can change the header's content with the '--label=label' option; see Section 2.2.4 [Alternate Names], page 14.

Next come one or more hunks of differences; each hunk shows one area where the files differ. Context format hunks look like this:

```
**************
*** from-file-line-numbers ****
  from-file-line
  from-file-line...
--- to-file-line-numbers ----
  to-file-line
  to-file-line...
```

If a hunk contains two or more lines, its line numbers look like '*start,end*'. Otherwise only its end line number appears. An empty hunk is considered to end at the line that precedes the hunk.

The lines of context around the lines that differ start with two space characters. The lines that differ between the two files start with one of the following indicator characters, followed by a space character:

'!'   A line that is part of a group of one or more lines that changed between the two files. There is a corresponding group of lines marked with '!' in the part of this hunk for the other file.

'+'   An "inserted" line in the second file that corresponds to nothing in the first file.

'-'   A "deleted" line in the first file that corresponds to nothing in the second file.

If all of the changes in a hunk are insertions, the lines of *from-file* are omitted. If all of the changes are deletions, the lines of *to-file* are omitted.

2.2.2 Unified Format

The unified output format is a variation on the context format that is more compact because it omits redundant context lines. To select this output format, use the '--unified[=*lines*]' ('-U *lines*'), or '-u' option. The argument *lines* is the number of lines of context to show. When it is not given, it defaults to three.

At present, only GNU diff can produce this format and only GNU patch can automatically apply diffs in this format. For proper operation, patch typically needs at least three lines of context.

2.2.2.1 An Example of Unified Format

Here is the output of the command 'diff -u lao tzu' (see Section 2.1 [Sample diff Input], page 9, for the complete contents of the two files):

```
--- lao 2002-02-21 23:30:39.942229878 -0800
+++ tzu 2002-02-21 23:30:50.442260588 -0800
@@ -1,7 +1,6 @@
-The Way that can be told of is not the eternal Way;
-The name that can be named is not the eternal name.
 The Nameless is the origin of Heaven and Earth;
-The Named is the mother of all things.
+The named is the mother of all things.
+
 Therefore let there always be non-being,
   so we may see their subtlety,
```

```
    And let there always be being,
 @@ -9,3 +8,6 @@
  The two are the same,
  But after they are produced,
    they have different names.
 +They both may be called deep and profound.
 +Deeper and more profound,
 +The door of all subtleties!
```

2.2.2.2 Detailed Description of Unified Format

The unified output format starts with a two-line header, which looks like this:

```
    --- from-file from-file-modification-time
    +++ to-file to-file-modification-time
```

The time stamp looks like '2002-02-21 23:30:39.942229878 -0800' to indicate the date, time with fractional seconds, and time zone. The fractional seconds are omitted on hosts that do not support fractional time stamps.

You can change the header's content with the '--label=label' option. See Section 2.2.4 [Alternate Names], page 14.

Next come one or more hunks of differences; each hunk shows one area where the files differ. Unified format hunks look like this:

```
    @@ from-file-line-numbers to-file-line-numbers @@
     line-from-either-file
     line-from-either-file...
```

If a hunk contains just one line, only its start line number appears. Otherwise its line numbers look like 'start,count'. An empty hunk is considered to start at the line that follows the hunk.

If a hunk and its context contain two or more lines, its line numbers look like 'start,count'. Otherwise only its end line number appears. An empty hunk is considered to end at the line that precedes the hunk.

The lines common to both files begin with a space character. The lines that actually differ between the two files have one of the following indicator characters in the left print column:

'+'   A line was added here to the first file.

'-'   A line was removed here from the first file.

2.2.3 Showing Which Sections Differences Are in

Sometimes you might want to know which part of the files each change falls in. If the files are source code, this could mean which function was changed. If the files are documents, it could mean which chapter or appendix was changed. GNU diff can show this by displaying the nearest section heading line that precedes the differing lines. Which lines are "section headings" is determined by a regular expression.

2.2.3.1 Showing Lines That Match Regular Expressions

To show in which sections differences occur for files that are not source code for C or similar languages, use the '`--show-function-line=`*regexp*' ('`-F `*regexp*') option. `diff` considers lines that match the `grep`-style regular expression *regexp* to be the beginning of a section of the file. Here are suggested regular expressions for some common languages:

'`^[[:alpha:]$_]`'
          C, C++, Prolog

'`^(`'   Lisp

'`^@node`'   Texinfo

This option does not automatically select an output format; in order to use it, you must select the context format (see Section 2.2.1 [Context Format], page 10) or unified format (see Section 2.2.2 [Unified Format], page 12). In other output formats it has no effect.

The '`--show-function-line`' ('`-F`') option finds the nearest unchanged line that precedes each hunk of differences and matches the given regular expression. Then it adds that line to the end of the line of asterisks in the context format, or to the '`@@`' line in unified format. If no matching line exists, this option leaves the output for that hunk unchanged. If that line is more than 40 characters long, it outputs only the first 40 characters. You can specify more than one regular expression for such lines; `diff` tries to match each line against each regular expression, starting with the last one given. This means that you can use '`-p`' and '`-F`' together, if you wish.

2.2.3.2 Showing C Function Headings

To show in which functions differences occur for C and similar languages, you can use the '`--show-c-function`' ('`-p`') option. This option automatically defaults to the context output format (see Section 2.2.1 [Context Format], page 10), with the default number of lines of context. You can override that number with '`-C `*lines*' elsewhere in the command line. You can override both the format and the number with '`-U `*lines*' elsewhere in the command line.

The '`--show-c-function`' ('`-p`') option is equivalent to '`-F '^[[:alpha:]$_]'`' if the unified format is specified, otherwise '`-c -F '^[[:alpha:]$_]'`' (see Section 2.2.3.1 [Specified Headings], page 14). GNU `diff` provides this option for the sake of convenience.

2.2.4 Showing Alternate File Names

If you are comparing two files that have meaningless or uninformative names, you might want `diff` to show alternate names in the header of the context and unified output formats. To do this, use the '`--label=`*label*' option. The first time you give this option, its argument replaces the name and date of the first file in the header; the second time, its argument replaces the name and date of the second file. If you give this option more than twice, `diff` reports an error. The '`--label`' option does not affect the file names in the `pr` header when the '`-l`' or '`--paginate`' option is used (see Section 5.3 [Pagination], page 31).

Here are the first two lines of the output from '`diff -C 2 --label=original --label=modified lao tzu`':

```
    *** original
    --- modified
```

2.3 Showing Differences Side by Side

diff can produce a side by side difference listing of two files. The files are listed in two columns with a gutter between them. The gutter contains one of the following markers:

white space

> The corresponding lines are in common. That is, either the lines are identical, or the difference is ignored because of one of the '--ignore' options (see Section 1.2 [White Space], page 4).

'|'

> The corresponding lines differ, and they are either both complete or both incomplete.

'<'

> The files differ and only the first file contains the line.

'>'

> The files differ and only the second file contains the line.

'('

> Only the first file contains the line, but the difference is ignored.

')'

> Only the second file contains the line, but the difference is ignored.

'\'

> The corresponding lines differ, and only the first line is incomplete.

'/'

> The corresponding lines differ, and only the second line is incomplete.

Normally, an output line is incomplete if and only if the lines that it contains are incomplete. See Chapter 3 [Incomplete Lines], page 27. However, when an output line represents two differing lines, one might be incomplete while the other is not. In this case, the output line is complete, but its the gutter is marked '\' if the first line is incomplete, '/' if the second line is.

Side by side format is sometimes easiest to read, but it has limitations. It generates much wider output than usual, and truncates lines that are too long to fit. Also, it relies on lining up output more heavily than usual, so its output looks particularly bad if you use varying width fonts, nonstandard tab stops, or nonprinting characters.

You can use the sdiff command to interactively merge side by side differences. See Chapter 9 [Interactive Merging], page 43, for more information on merging files.

2.3.1 Controlling Side by Side Format

The '--side-by-side' ('-y') option selects side by side format. Because side by side output lines contain two input lines, the output is wider than usual: normally 130 print columns, which can fit onto a traditional printer line. You can set the width of the output with the '--width=columns' ('-W columns') option. The output is split into two halves of equal width, separated by a small gutter to mark differences; the right half is aligned to a tab stop so that tabs line up. Input lines that are too long to fit in half of an output line are truncated for output.

The '--left-column' option prints only the left column of two common lines. The '--suppress-common-lines' option suppresses common lines entirely.

2.3.2 An Example of Side by Side Format

Here is the output of the command 'diff -y -W 72 lao tzu' (see Section 2.1 [Sample diff Input], page 9, for the complete contents of the two files).

```
The Way that can be told of is n    <
The name that can be named is no    <
The Nameless is the origin of He             The Nameless is the origin of He
The Named is the mother of all t    |        The named is the mother of all t
                                    >

Therefore let there always be no             Therefore let there always be no
  so we may see their subtlety,                so we may see their subtlety,
And let there always be being,               And let there always be being,
  so we may see their outcome.                 so we may see their outcome.
The two are the same,                        The two are the same,
But after they are produced,                 But after they are produced,
  they have different names.                   they have different names.
                                    >        They both may be called deep and
                                    >        Deeper and more profound,
                                    >        The door of all subtleties!
```

2.4 Showing Differences Without Context

The "normal" diff output format shows each hunk of differences without any surrounding context. Sometimes such output is the clearest way to see how lines have changed, without the clutter of nearby unchanged lines (although you can get similar results with the context or unified formats by using 0 lines of context). However, this format is no longer widely used for sending out patches; for that purpose, the context format (see Section 2.2.1 [Context Format], page 10) and the unified format (see Section 2.2.2 [Unified Format], page 12) are superior. Normal format is the default for compatibility with older versions of diff and the POSIX standard. Use the '--normal' option to select this output format explicitly.

2.4.1 An Example of Normal Format

Here is the output of the command 'diff lao tzu' (see Section 2.1 [Sample diff Input], page 9, for the complete contents of the two files). Notice that it shows only the lines that are different between the two files.

```
1,2d0
< The Way that can be told of is not the eternal Way;
< The name that can be named is not the eternal name.
4c2,3
< The Named is the mother of all things.
---
> The named is the mother of all things.
>
11a11,13
> They both may be called deep and profound.
> Deeper and more profound,
> The door of all subtleties!
```

2.4.2 Detailed Description of Normal Format

The normal output format consists of one or more hunks of differences; each hunk shows one area where the files differ. Normal format hunks look like this:

```
change-command
< from-file-line
< from-file-line...
---
> to-file-line
> to-file-line...
```

There are three types of change commands. Each consists of a line number or comma-separated range of lines in the first file, a single character indicating the kind of change to make, and a line number or comma-separated range of lines in the second file. All line numbers are the original line numbers in each file. The types of change commands are:

'*l*a*r*'   Add the lines in range *r* of the second file after line *l* of the first file. For example, '8a12,15' means append lines 12–15 of file 2 after line 8 of file 1; or, if changing file 2 into file 1, delete lines 12–15 of file 2.

'*f*c*t*'   Replace the lines in range *f* of the first file with lines in range *t* of the second file. This is like a combined add and delete, but more compact. For example, '5,7c8,10' means change lines 5–7 of file 1 to read as lines 8–10 of file 2; or, if changing file 2 into file 1, change lines 8–10 of file 2 to read as lines 5–7 of file 1.

'*r*d*l*'   Delete the lines in range *r* from the first file; line *l* is where they would have appeared in the second file had they not been deleted. For example, '5,7d3' means delete lines 5–7 of file 1; or, if changing file 2 into file 1, append lines 5–7 of file 1 after line 3 of file 2.

2.5 Making Edit Scripts

Several output modes produce command scripts for editing *from-file* to produce *to-file*.

2.5.1 `ed` Scripts

`diff` can produce commands that direct the **ed** text editor to change the first file into the second file. Long ago, this was the only output mode that was suitable for editing one file into another automatically; today, with **patch**, it is almost obsolete. Use the '--ed' ('-e') option to select this output format.

Like the normal format (see Section 2.4 [Normal], page 16), this output format does not show any context; unlike the normal format, it does not include the information necessary to apply the diff in reverse (to produce the first file if all you have is the second file and the diff).

If the file 'd' contains the output of 'diff -e old new', then the command '(cat d && echo w) | ed - old' edits 'old' to make it a copy of 'new'. More generally, if 'd1', 'd2', ..., 'dN' contain the outputs of 'diff -e old new1', 'diff -e new1 new2', ..., 'diff -e newN-1 newN', respectively, then the command '(cat d1 d2 ... dN && echo w) | ed - old' edits 'old' to make it a copy of 'newN'.

2.5.1.1 Example `ed` Script

Here is the output of 'diff -e lao tzu' (see Section 2.1 [Sample diff Input], page 9, for the complete contents of the two files):

```
11a
They both may be called deep and profound.
Deeper and more profound,
The door of all subtleties!
.
4c
The named is the mother of all things.

.
1,2d
```

2.5.1.2 Detailed Description of ed Format

The `ed` output format consists of one or more hunks of differences. The changes closest to the ends of the files come first so that commands that change the number of lines do not affect how `ed` interprets line numbers in succeeding commands. `ed` format hunks look like this:

```
change-command
to-file-line
to-file-line...
.
```

Because `ed` uses a single period on a line to indicate the end of input, GNU `diff` protects lines of changes that contain a single period on a line by writing two periods instead, then writing a subsequent `ed` command to change the two periods into one. The `ed` format cannot represent an incomplete line, so if the second file ends in a changed incomplete line, `diff` reports an error and then pretends that a newline was appended.

There are three types of change commands. Each consists of a line number or comma-separated range of lines in the first file and a single character indicating the kind of change to make. All line numbers are the original line numbers in the file. The types of change commands are:

'la'   Add text from the second file after line l in the first file. For example, '8a' means to add the following lines after line 8 of file 1.

'rc'   Replace the lines in range r in the first file with the following lines. Like a combined add and delete, but more compact. For example, '5,7c' means change lines 5–7 of file 1 to read as the text file 2.

'rd'   Delete the lines in range r from the first file. For example, '5,7d' means delete lines 5–7 of file 1.

2.5.2 Forward ed Scripts

`diff` can produce output that is like an `ed` script, but with hunks in forward (front to back) order. The format of the commands is also changed slightly: command characters precede the lines they modify, spaces separate line numbers in ranges, and no attempt is made to disambiguate hunk lines consisting of a single period. Like `ed` format, forward `ed` format cannot represent incomplete lines.

Forward `ed` format is not very useful, because neither `ed` nor `patch` can apply diffs in this format. It exists mainly for compatibility with older versions of `diff`. Use the '-f' or '--forward-ed' option to select it.

2.5.3 RCS Scripts

The RCS output format is designed specifically for use by the Revision Control System, which is a set of free programs used for organizing different versions and systems of files. Use the '--rcs' ('-n') option to select this output format. It is like the forward `ed` format (see Section 2.5.2 [Forward ed], page 18), but it can represent arbitrary changes to the contents of a file because it avoids the forward `ed` format's problems with lines consisting of a single period and with incomplete lines. Instead of ending text sections with a line consisting of a single period, each command specifies the number of lines it affects; a combination of the 'a' and 'd' commands are used instead of 'c'. Also, if the second file ends in a changed incomplete line, then the output also ends in an incomplete line.

Here is the output of 'diff -n lao tzu' (see Section 2.1 [Sample diff Input], page 9, for the complete contents of the two files):

```
d1 2
d4 1
a4 2
The named is the mother of all things.

a11 3
They both may be called deep and profound.
Deeper and more profound,
The door of all subtleties!
```

2.6 Merging Files with If-then-else

You can use `diff` to merge two files of C source code. The output of `diff` in this format contains all the lines of both files. Lines common to both files are output just once; the differing parts are separated by the C preprocessor directives `#ifdef name` or `#ifndef name`, `#else`, and `#endif`. When compiling the output, you select which version to use by either defining or leaving undefined the macro *name*.

To merge two files, use `diff` with the '-D name' or '--ifdef=name' option. The argument *name* is the C preprocessor identifier to use in the `#ifdef` and `#ifndef` directives.

For example, if you change an instance of `wait (&s)` to `waitpid (-1, &s, 0)` and then merge the old and new files with the '--ifdef=HAVE_WAITPID' option, then the affected part of your code might look like this:

```
    do {
#ifndef HAVE_WAITPID
        if ((w = wait (&s)) < 0  &&  errno != EINTR)
#else /* HAVE_WAITPID */
        if ((w = waitpid (-1, &s, 0)) < 0  &&  errno != EINTR)
#endif /* HAVE_WAITPID */
            return w;
    } while (w != child);
```

You can specify formats for languages other than C by using line group formats and line formats, as described in the next sections.

2.6.1 Line Group Formats

Line group formats let you specify formats suitable for many applications that allow if-then-else input, including programming languages and text formatting languages. A line group format specifies the output format for a contiguous group of similar lines.

For example, the following command compares the TeX files 'old' and 'new', and outputs a merged file in which old regions are surrounded by '\begin{em}'-'\end{em}' lines, and new regions are surrounded by '\begin{bf}'-'\end{bf}' lines.

```
diff \
    --old-group-format='\begin{em}
%<\end{em}
' \
    --new-group-format='\begin{bf}
%>\end{bf}
' \
    old new
```

The following command is equivalent to the above example, but it is a little more verbose, because it spells out the default line group formats.

```
diff \
    --old-group-format='\begin{em}
%<\end{em}
' \
    --new-group-format='\begin{bf}
%>\end{bf}
' \
    --unchanged-group-format='%=' \
    --changed-group-format='\begin{em}
%<\end{em}
\begin{bf}
%>\end{bf}
' \
    old new
```

Here is a more advanced example, which outputs a diff listing with headers containing line numbers in a "plain English" style.

```
diff \
    --unchanged-group-format='' \
    --old-group-format='-------- %dn line%(n=1?:s) deleted at %df:
%<' \
    --new-group-format='-------- %dN line%(N=1?:s) added after %de:
%>' \
    --changed-group-format='-------- %dn line%(n=1?:s) changed at %df:
%<-------- to:
%>' \
```

       old new

To specify a line group format, use diff with one of the options listed below. You can specify up to four line group formats, one for each kind of line group. You should quote *format*, because it typically contains shell metacharacters.

'--old-group-format=*format*'

> These line groups are hunks containing only lines from the first file. The default old group format is the same as the changed group format if it is specified; otherwise it is a format that outputs the line group as-is.

'--new-group-format=*format*'

> These line groups are hunks containing only lines from the second file. The default new group format is same as the changed group format if it is specified; otherwise it is a format that outputs the line group as-is.

'--changed-group-format=*format*'

> These line groups are hunks containing lines from both files. The default changed group format is the concatenation of the old and new group formats.

'--unchanged-group-format=*format*'

> These line groups contain lines common to both files. The default unchanged group format is a format that outputs the line group as-is.

In a line group format, ordinary characters represent themselves; conversion specifications start with '%' and have one of the following forms.

'%<'   stands for the lines from the first file, including the trailing newline. Each line is formatted according to the old line format (see Section 2.6.2 [Line Formats], page 22).

'%>'   stands for the lines from the second file, including the trailing newline. Each line is formatted according to the new line format.

'%='   stands for the lines common to both files, including the trailing newline. Each line is formatted according to the unchanged line format.

'%%'   stands for '%'.

'%c'*C*''   where *C* is a single character, stands for *C*. *C* may not be a backslash or an apostrophe. For example, '%c':'' stands for a colon, even inside the then-part of an if-then-else format, which a colon would normally terminate.

'%c'*O*''   where *O* is a string of 1, 2, or 3 octal digits, stands for the character with octal code *O*. For example, '%c'\0'' stands for a null character.

'*Fn*'   where *F* is a printf conversion specification and *n* is one of the following letters, stands for *n*'s value formatted with *F*.

> 'e'   The line number of the line just before the group in the old file.
>
> 'f'   The line number of the first line in the group in the old file; equals $e + 1$.
>
> 'l'   The line number of the last line in the group in the old file.

'm'   The line number of the line just after the group in the old file; equals l + 1.

'n'   The number of lines in the group in the old file; equals l - f + 1.

'E, F, L, M, N'
                Likewise, for lines in the new file.

The `printf` conversion specification can be '%d', '%o', '%x', or '%X', specifying decimal, octal, lower case hexadecimal, or upper case hexadecimal output respectively. After the '%' the following options can appear in sequence: a series of zero or more flags; an integer specifying the minimum field width; and a period followed by an optional integer specifying the minimum number of digits. The flags are '-' for left-justification, '' ' for separating the digit into groups as specified by the `LC_NUMERIC` locale category, and '0' for padding with zeros instead of spaces. For example, '%5dN' prints the number of new lines in the group in a field of width 5 characters, using the `printf` format "%5d".

'(A=B?T:E)'
                If A equals B then T else E. A and B are each either a decimal constant or a single letter interpreted as above. This format spec is equivalent to T if A's value equals B's; otherwise it is equivalent to E.

                For example, '%(N=0?no:%dN) line%(N=1?:s)' is equivalent to 'no lines' if N (the number of lines in the group in the new file) is 0, to '1 line' if N is 1, and to '%dN lines' otherwise.

2.6.2 Line Formats

Line formats control how each line taken from an input file is output as part of a line group in if-then-else format.

For example, the following command outputs text with a one-character change indicator to the left of the text. The first character of output is '-' for deleted lines, '|' for added lines, and a space for unchanged lines. The formats contain newline characters where newlines are desired on output.

```
diff \
    --old-line-format='-%l
' \
    --new-line-format='|%l
' \
    --unchanged-line-format=' %l
' \
    old new
```

To specify a line format, use one of the following options. You should quote *format*, since it often contains shell metacharacters.

'--old-line-format=*format*'
                formats lines just from the first file.

'--new-line-format=*format*'
                formats lines just from the second file.

'`--unchanged-line-format=`*format*'
>	formats lines common to both files.

'`--line-format=`*format*'
>	formats all lines; in effect, it sets all three above options simultaneously.

In a line format, ordinary characters represent themselves; conversion specifications start with '%' and have one of the following forms.

'`%l`'
>	stands for the contents of the line, not counting its trailing newline (if any). This format ignores whether the line is incomplete; See Chapter 3 [Incomplete Lines], page 27.

'`%L`'
>	stands for the contents of the line, including its trailing newline (if any). If a line is incomplete, this format preserves its incompleteness.

'`%%`'
>	stands for '%'.

'`%c'`*C*`'`'
>	where *C* is a single character, stands for *C*. *C* may not be a backslash or an apostrophe. For example, '`%c':''` stands for a colon.

'`%c'\`*O*`'`'
>	where *O* is a string of 1, 2, or 3 octal digits, stands for the character with octal code *O*. For example, '`%c'\0''` stands for a null character.

'`F`*n*'
>	where *F* is a `printf` conversion specification, stands for the line number formatted with *F*. For example, '`%.5d`*n*' prints the line number using the `printf` format "`%.5d`". See Section 2.6.1 [Line Group Formats], page 20, for more about printf conversion specifications.

The default line format is '`%l`' followed by a newline character.

If the input contains tab characters and it is important that they line up on output, you should ensure that '`%l`' or '`%L`' in a line format is just after a tab stop (e.g. by preceding '`%l`' or '`%L`' with a tab character), or you should use the '`-t`' or '`--expand-tabs`' option.

Taken together, the line and line group formats let you specify many different formats. For example, the following command uses a format similar to normal `diff` format. You can tailor this command to get fine control over `diff` output.

```
diff \
   --old-line-format='< %l
' \
   --new-line-format='> %l
' \
   --old-group-format='%df%(f=1?:,%dl)d%dE
%<' \
   --new-group-format='%dea%dF%(F=L?:,%dL)
%>' \
   --changed-group-format='%df%(f=1?:,%dl)c%dF%(F=L?:,%dL)
%<---
%>' \
   --unchanged-group-format='' \
   old new
```

2.6.3 An Example of If-then-else Format

Here is the output of 'diff -DTWO lao tzu' (see Section 2.1 [Sample diff Input], page 9, for the complete contents of the two files):

```
#ifndef TWO
The Way that can be told of is not the eternal Way;
The name that can be named is not the eternal name.
#endif /* ! TWO */
The Nameless is the origin of Heaven and Earth;
#ifndef TWO
The Named is the mother of all things.
#else /* TWO */
The named is the mother of all things.

#endif /* TWO */
Therefore let there always be non-being,
  so we may see their subtlety,
And let there always be being,
  so we may see their outcome.
The two are the same,
But after they are produced,
  they have different names.
#ifdef TWO
They both may be called deep and profound.
Deeper and more profound,
The door of all subtleties!
#endif /* TWO */
```

2.6.4 Detailed Description of If-then-else Format

For lines common to both files, diff uses the unchanged line group format. For each hunk of differences in the merged output format, if the hunk contains only lines from the first file, diff uses the old line group format; if the hunk contains only lines from the second file, diff uses the new group format; otherwise, diff uses the changed group format.

The old, new, and unchanged line formats specify the output format of lines from the first file, lines from the second file, and lines common to both files, respectively.

The option '--ifdef=name' is equivalent to the following sequence of options using shell syntax:

```
--old-group-format='#ifndef name
%<#endif /* ! name */
' \
--new-group-format='#ifdef name
%>#endif /* name */
' \
--unchanged-group-format='%=' \
--changed-group-format='#ifndef name
%<#else /* name */
```

```
%>#endif /* name */
```
,

You should carefully check the `diff` output for proper nesting. For example, when using the '`-D name`' or '`--ifdef=name`' option, you should check that if the differing lines contain any of the C preprocessor directives '`#ifdef`', '`#ifndef`', '`#else`', '`#elif`', or '`#endif`', they are nested properly and match. If they don't, you must make corrections manually. It is a good idea to carefully check the resulting code anyway to make sure that it really does what you want it to; depending on how the input files were produced, the output might contain duplicate or otherwise incorrect code.

The `patch` '`-D name`' option behaves like the `diff` '`-D name`' option, except it operates on a file and a diff to produce a merged file. See Section 15.1 [patch Options], page 69.

3 Incomplete Lines

When an input file ends in a non-newline character, its last line is called an *incomplete line* because its last character is not a newline. All other lines are called *full lines* and end in a newline character. Incomplete lines do not match full lines unless differences in white space are ignored (see Section 1.2 [White Space], page 4).

An incomplete line is normally distinguished on output from a full line by a following line that starts with '\'. However, the RCS format (see Section 2.5.3 [RCS], page 19) outputs the incomplete line as-is, without any trailing newline or following line. The side by side format normally represents incomplete lines as-is, but in some cases uses a '\' or '/' gutter marker. See Section 2.3 [Side by Side], page 15. The if-then-else line format preserves a line's incompleteness with '%L', and discards the newline with '%l'. See Section 2.6.2 [Line Formats], page 22. Finally, with the **ed** and forward **ed** output formats (see Chapter 2 [Output Formats], page 9) **diff** cannot represent an incomplete line, so it pretends there was a newline and reports an error.

For example, suppose 'F' and 'G' are one-byte files that contain just 'f' and 'g', respectively. Then 'diff F G' outputs

```
1c1
< f
\ No newline at end of file
---
> g
\ No newline at end of file
```

(The exact message may differ in non-English locales.) 'diff -n F G' outputs the following without a trailing newline:

```
d1 1
a1 1
g
```

'diff -e F G' reports two errors and outputs the following:

```
1c
g
.
```

4 Comparing Directories

You can use `diff` to compare some or all of the files in two directory trees. When both file name arguments to `diff` are directories, it compares each file that is contained in both directories, examining file names in alphabetical order as specified by the `LC_COLLATE` locale category. Normally `diff` is silent about pairs of files that contain no differences, but if you use the '`--report-identical-files`' ('`-s`') option, it reports pairs of identical files. Normally `diff` reports subdirectories common to both directories without comparing subdirectories' files, but if you use the '`-r`' or '`--recursive`' option, it compares every corresponding pair of files in the directory trees, as many levels deep as they go.

If only one file exists, `diff` normally does not show its contents; it merely reports that one file exists but the other does not. You can make `diff` act as though the missing file is empty, so that it outputs the entire contents of the file that actually exists. (It is output as either an insertion or a deletion, depending on whether the missing file is in the first or the second position.) To do this, use the '`--new-file`' ('`-N`') option. This option affects command-line arguments as well as files found via directory traversal; for example, '`diff -N a b`' treats '`a`' as empty if '`a`' does not exist but '`b`' does, and similarly '`diff -N - b`' treats standard input as empty if it is closed but '`b`' exists.

If the older directory contains large files that are not in the newer directory, you can make the patch smaller by using the '`--unidirectional-new-file`' option instead of '`-N`'. This option is like '`-N`' except that it inserts the contents only of files that appear in the second directory but not the first (that is, files that were added). At the top of the patch, write instructions for the user applying the patch to remove the files that were deleted before applying the patch. See Chapter 11 [Making Patches], page 55, for more discussion of making patches for distribution.

To ignore some files while comparing directories, use the '`--exclude=pattern`' ('`-x pattern`') option. This option ignores any files or subdirectories whose base names match the shell pattern *pattern*. Unlike in the shell, a period at the start of the base of a file name matches a wildcard at the start of a pattern. You should enclose *pattern* in quotes so that the shell does not expand it. For example, the option '`-x '*.[ao]'`' ignores any file whose name ends with '`.a`' or '`.o`'.

This option accumulates if you specify it more than once. For example, using the options '`-x 'RCS' -x '*,v'`' ignores any file or subdirectory whose base name is '`RCS`' or ends with '`,v`'.

If you need to give this option many times, you can instead put the patterns in a file, one pattern per line, and use the '`--exclude-from=file`' ('`-X file`') option. Trailing white space and empty lines are ignored in the pattern file.

If you have been comparing two directories and stopped partway through, later you might want to continue where you left off. You can do this by using the '`--starting-file=file`' ('`-S file`') option. This compares only the file *file* and all alphabetically later files in the topmost directory level.

If two directories differ only in that file names are lower case in one directory and upper case in the upper, `diff` normally reports many differences because it compares file names in a case sensitive way. With the '`--ignore-file-name-case`' option, `diff` ignores case differences in file names, so that for example the contents of the file '`Tao`' in one directory are compared to the contents of the file 'TAO' in the other. The '--no-ignore-file-name-case' option cancels the effect of the '--ignore-file-name-case' option, reverting to the default behavior.

If an '--exclude=pattern' ('-x pattern') option, or an '--exclude-from=file' ('-X file') option, is specified while the '--ignore-file-name-case' option is in effect, case is ignored when excluding file names matching the specified patterns.

To avoid that diff follows symbolic links, use the '--no-dereference'. When this option is in use, symbolic links will be treated like a special kind of files, rather than comparing the target of each symbolic link.

5 Making `diff` Output Prettier

`diff` provides several ways to adjust the appearance of its output. These adjustments can be applied to any output format.

5.1 Preserving Tab Stop Alignment

The lines of text in some of the `diff` output formats are preceded by one or two characters that indicate whether the text is inserted, deleted, or changed. The addition of those characters can cause tabs to move to the next tab stop, throwing off the alignment of columns in the line. GNU `diff` provides two ways to make tab-aligned columns line up correctly.

The first way is to have `diff` convert all tabs into the correct number of spaces before outputting them; select this method with the '`--expand-tabs`' ('`-t`') option. To use this form of output with `patch`, you must give `patch` the '`-l`' or '`--ignore-white-space`' option (see Section 10.3.1 [Changed White Space], page 46, for more information). `diff` normally assumes that tab stops are set every 8 print columns, but this can be altered by the '`--tabsize=columns`' option.

The other method for making tabs line up correctly is to add a tab character instead of a space after the indicator character at the beginning of the line. This ensures that all following tab characters are in the same position relative to tab stops that they were in the original files, so that the output is aligned correctly. Its disadvantage is that it can make long lines too long to fit on one line of the screen or the paper. It also does not work with the unified output format, which does not have a space character after the change type indicator character. Select this method with the '`-T`' or '`--initial-tab`' option.

5.2 Omitting trailing blanks

When outputting lines in normal or context format, or outputting an unchanged line in unified format, `diff` normally outputs a blank just before each line. If the line is empty, the output of `diff` therefore contains trailing blanks even though the input does not contain them. For example, when outputting an unchanged empty line in context format, `diff` normally outputs a line with two leading spaces.

Some text editors and email agents routinely delete trailing blanks, so it can be a problem to deal with diff output files that contain them. You can avoid this problem with the '`--suppress-blank-empty`' option. It causes `diff` to omit trailing blanks at the end of output lines in normal, context, and unified format, unless the trailing blanks were already present in the input. This changes the output format slightly, so that output lines are guaranteed to never end in a blank unless an input line ends in a blank. This format is less likely to be munged by text editors or by transmission via email. It is accepted by GNU `patch` as well.

5.3 Paginating `diff` Output

It can be convenient to have long output page-numbered and time-stamped. The '`--paginate`' ('`-l`') option does this by sending the `diff` output through the `pr` program. Here is what the page header might look like for '`diff -lc lao tzu`':

```
2002-02-22 14:20              diff -lc lao tzu              Page 1
```

6 `diff` Performance Tradeoffs

GNU `diff` runs quite efficiently; however, in some circumstances you can cause it to run faster or produce a more compact set of changes.

One way to improve `diff` performance is to use hard or symbolic links to files instead of copies. This improves performance because `diff` normally does not need to read two hard or symbolic links to the same file, since their contents must be identical. For example, suppose you copy a large directory hierarchy, make a few changes to the copy, and then often use 'diff -r' to compare the original to the copy. If the original files are read-only, you can greatly improve performance by creating the copy using hard or symbolic links (e.g., with GNU 'cp -lR' or 'cp -sR'). Before editing a file in the copy for the first time, you should break the link and replace it with a regular copy.

You can also affect the performance of GNU `diff` by giving it options that change the way it compares files. Performance has more than one dimension. These options improve one aspect of performance at the cost of another, or they improve performance in some cases while hurting it in others.

The way that GNU `diff` determines which lines have changed always comes up with a near-minimal set of differences. Usually it is good enough for practical purposes. If the `diff` output is large, you might want `diff` to use a modified algorithm that sometimes produces a smaller set of differences. The '--minimal' ('-d') option does this; however, it can also cause `diff` to run more slowly than usual, so it is not the default behavior.

When the files you are comparing are large and have small groups of changes scattered throughout them, you can use the '--speed-large-files' option to make a different modification to the algorithm that `diff` uses. If the input files have a constant small density of changes, this option speeds up the comparisons without changing the output. If not, `diff` might produce a larger set of differences; however, the output will still be correct.

Normally `diff` discards the prefix and suffix that is common to both files before it attempts to find a minimal set of differences. This makes `diff` run faster, but occasionally it may produce non-minimal output. The '--horizon-lines=*lines*' option prevents `diff` from discarding the last *lines* lines of the prefix and the first *lines* lines of the suffix. This gives `diff` further opportunities to find a minimal output.

Suppose a run of changed lines includes a sequence of lines at one end and there is an identical sequence of lines just outside the other end. The `diff` command is free to choose which identical sequence is included in the hunk. In this case, `diff` normally shifts the hunk's boundaries when this merges adjacent hunks, or shifts a hunk's lines towards the end of the file. Merging hunks can make the output look nicer in some cases.

7 Comparing Three Files

Use the program `diff3` to compare three files and show any differences among them. (`diff3` can also merge files; see Chapter 8 [diff3 Merging], page 39).

The "normal" `diff3` output format shows each hunk of differences without surrounding context. Hunks are labeled depending on whether they are two-way or three-way, and lines are annotated by their location in the input files.

See Chapter 14 [Invoking diff3], page 67, for more information on how to run `diff3`.

7.1 A Third Sample Input File

Here is a third sample file that will be used in examples to illustrate the output of `diff3` and how various options can change it. The first two files are the same that we used for `diff` (see Section 2.1 [Sample diff Input], page 9). This is the third sample file, called 'tao':

```
The Way that can be told of is not the eternal Way;
The name that can be named is not the eternal name.
The Nameless is the origin of Heaven and Earth;
The named is the mother of all things.

Therefore let there always be non-being,
  so we may see their subtlety,
And let there always be being,
  so we may see their result.
The two are the same,
But after they are produced,
  they have different names.

    -- The Way of Lao-Tzu, tr. Wing-tsit Chan
```

7.2 An Example of `diff3` Normal Format

Here is the output of the command 'diff3 lao tzu tao' (see Section 7.1 [Sample diff3 Input], page 35, for the complete contents of the files). Notice that it shows only the lines that are different among the three files.

```
====2
1:1,2c
3:1,2c
  The Way that can be told of is not the eternal Way;
  The name that can be named is not the eternal name.
2:0a
====1
1:4c
  The Named is the mother of all things.
2:2,3c
3:4,5c
  The named is the mother of all things.
```

```
====3
1:8c
2:7c
      so we may see their outcome.
3:9c
      so we may see their result.
====
1:11a
2:11,13c
   They both may be called deep and profound.
   Deeper and more profound,
   The door of all subtleties!
3:13,14c

      -- The Way of Lao-Tzu, tr. Wing-tsit Chan
```

7.3 Detailed Description of `diff3` Normal Format

Each hunk begins with a line marked '===='. Three-way hunks have plain '====' lines, and two-way hunks have '1', '2', or '3' appended to specify which of the three input files differ in that hunk. The hunks contain copies of two or three sets of input lines each preceded by one or two commands identifying where the lines came from.

Normally, two spaces precede each copy of an input line to distinguish it from the commands. But with the '`--initial-tab`' ('`-T`') option, `diff3` uses a tab instead of two spaces; this lines up tabs correctly. See Section 5.1 [Tabs], page 31, for more information.

Commands take the following forms:

'`file:1a`' This hunk appears after line *l* of file *file*, and contains no lines in that file. To edit this file to yield the other files, one must append hunk lines taken from the other files. For example, '`1:11a`' means that the hunk follows line 11 in the first file and contains no lines from that file.

'`file:rc`' This hunk contains the lines in the range *r* of file *file*. The range *r* is a comma-separated pair of line numbers, or just one number if there is only one line. To edit this file to yield the other files, one must change the specified lines to be the lines taken from the other files. For example, '`2:11,13c`' means that the hunk contains lines 11 through 13 from the second file.

If the last line in a set of input lines is incomplete (see Chapter 3 [Incomplete Lines], page 27), it is distinguished on output from a full line by a following line that starts with '\'.

7.4 `diff3` Hunks

Groups of lines that differ in two or three of the input files are called *diff3 hunks*, by analogy with `diff` hunks (see Section 1.1 [Hunks], page 3). If all three input files differ in a `diff3` hunk, the hunk is called a *three-way hunk*; if just two input files differ, it is a *two-way hunk*.

As with `diff`, several solutions are possible. When comparing the files 'A', 'B', and 'C', `diff3` normally finds `diff3` hunks by merging the two-way hunks output by the two commands 'diff A B' and 'diff A C'. This does not necessarily minimize the size of the output, but exceptions should be rare.

For example, suppose 'F' contains the three lines 'a', 'b', 'f', 'G' contains the lines 'g', 'b', 'g', and 'H' contains the lines 'a', 'b', 'h'. 'diff3 F G H' might output the following:

```
====2
1:1c
3:1c
  a
2:1c
  g
====
1:3c
  f
2:3c
  g
3:3c
  h
```

because it found a two-way hunk containing 'a' in the first and third files and 'g' in the second file, then the single line 'b' common to all three files, then a three-way hunk containing the last line of each file.

8 Merging From a Common Ancestor

When two people have made changes to copies of the same file, diff3 can produce a merged output that contains both sets of changes together with warnings about conflicts.

One might imagine programs with names like diff4 and diff5 to compare more than three files simultaneously, but in practice the need rarely arises. You can use diff3 to merge three or more sets of changes to a file by merging two change sets at a time.

diff3 can incorporate changes from two modified versions into a common preceding version. This lets you merge the sets of changes represented by the two newer files. Specify the common ancestor version as the second argument and the two newer versions as the first and third arguments, like this:

    diff3 *mine older yours*

You can remember the order of the arguments by noting that they are in alphabetical order.

You can think of this as subtracting *older* from *yours* and adding the result to *mine*, or as merging into *mine* the changes that would turn *older* into *yours*. This merging is well-defined as long as *mine* and *older* match in the neighborhood of each such change. This fails to be true when all three input files differ or when only *older* differs; we call this a *conflict*. When all three input files differ, we call the conflict an *overlap*.

diff3 gives you several ways to handle overlaps and conflicts. You can omit overlaps or conflicts, or select only overlaps, or mark conflicts with special '<<<<<<<' and '>>>>>>>' lines.

diff3 can output the merge results as an ed script that that can be applied to the first file to yield the merged output. However, it is usually better to have diff3 generate the merged output directly; this bypasses some problems with ed.

8.1 Selecting Which Changes to Incorporate

You can select all unmerged changes from *older* to *yours* for merging into *mine* with the '--ed' ('-e') option. You can select only the nonoverlapping unmerged changes with '--easy-only' ('-3'), and you can select only the overlapping changes with '--overlap-only' ('-x').

The '-e', '-3' and '-x' options select only *unmerged changes*, i.e. changes where *mine* and *yours* differ; they ignore changes from *older* to *yours* where *mine* and *yours* are identical, because they assume that such changes have already been merged. If this assumption is not a safe one, you can use the '--show-all' ('-A') option (see Section 8.2 [Marking Conflicts], page 40).

Here is the output of the command diff3 with each of these three options (see Section 7.1 [Sample diff3 Input], page 35, for the complete contents of the files). Notice that '-e' outputs the union of the disjoint sets of changes output by '-3' and '-x'.

Output of 'diff3 -e lao tzu tao':

    11a

      -- The Way of Lao-Tzu, tr. Wing-tsit Chan

    .
    8c

```
    so we may see their result.
      .
```

Output of 'diff3 -3 lao tzu tao':

```
    8c
      so we may see their result.
      .
```

Output of 'diff3 -x lao tzu tao':

```
    11a

      -- The Way of Lao-Tzu, tr. Wing-tsit Chan
      .
```

8.2 Marking Conflicts

diff3 can mark conflicts in the merged output by bracketing them with special marker lines. A conflict that comes from two files *A* and *B* is marked as follows:

```
<<<<<<< A
lines from A
=======
lines from B
>>>>>>> B
```

A conflict that comes from three files *A*, *B* and *C* is marked as follows:

```
<<<<<<< A
lines from A
||||||| B
lines from B
=======
lines from C
>>>>>>> C
```

The '--show-all' ('-A') option acts like the '-e' option, except that it brackets conflicts, and it outputs all changes from *older* to *yours*, not just the unmerged changes. Thus, given the sample input files (see Section 7.1 [Sample diff3 Input], page 35), 'diff3 -A lao tzu tao' puts brackets around the conflict where only 'tzu' differs:

```
<<<<<<< tzu
=======
The Way that can be told of is not the eternal Way;
The name that can be named is not the eternal name.
>>>>>>> tao
```

And it outputs the three-way conflict as follows:

```
<<<<<<< lao
||||||| tzu
They both may be called deep and profound.
Deeper and more profound,
The door of all subtleties!
=======
```

```
        -- The Way of Lao-Tzu, tr. Wing-tsit Chan
     >>>>>>> tao
```

The '--show-overlap' ('-E') option outputs less information than the '--show-all' ('-A') option, because it outputs only unmerged changes, and it never outputs the contents of the second file. Thus the '-E' option acts like the '-e' option, except that it brackets the first and third files from three-way overlapping changes. Similarly, '-X' acts like '-x', except it brackets all its (necessarily overlapping) changes. For example, for the three-way overlapping change above, the '-E' and '-X' options output the following:

```
     <<<<<<< lao
     =======
```

```
        -- The Way of Lao-Tzu, tr. Wing-tsit Chan
     >>>>>>> tao
```

If you are comparing files that have meaningless or uninformative names, you can use the '--label=label' option to show alternate names in the '<<<<<<<', '|||||||' and '>>>>>>>' brackets. This option can be given up to three times, once for each input file. Thus 'diff3 -A --label X --label Y --label Z A B C' acts like 'diff3 -A A B C', except that the output looks like it came from files named 'X', 'Y' and 'Z' rather than from files named 'A', 'B' and 'C'.

8.3 Generating the Merged Output Directly

With the '--merge' ('-m') option, diff3 outputs the merged file directly. This is more efficient than using ed to generate it, and works even with non-text files that ed would reject. If you specify '-m' without an ed script option, '-A' is assumed.

For example, the command 'diff3 -m lao tzu tao' (see Section 7.1 [Sample diff3 Input], page 35 for a copy of the input files) would output the following:

```
     <<<<<<< tzu
     =======
     The Way that can be told of is not the eternal Way;
     The name that can be named is not the eternal name.
     >>>>>>> tao
     The Nameless is the origin of Heaven and Earth;
     The Named is the mother of all things.
     Therefore let there always be non-being,
       so we may see their subtlety,
     And let there always be being,
       so we may see their result.
     The two are the same,
     But after they are produced,
       they have different names.
     <<<<<<< lao
     ||||||| tzu
     They both may be called deep and profound.
     Deeper and more profound,
```

```
The door of all subtleties!
=======

    -- The Way of Lao-Tzu, tr. Wing-tsit Chan
>>>>>>> tao
```

8.4 How `diff3` Merges Incomplete Lines

With '`-m`', incomplete lines (see Chapter 3 [Incomplete Lines], page 27) are simply copied to the output as they are found; if the merged output ends in an conflict and one of the input files ends in an incomplete line, succeeding '`| | | | | | |`', '`=======`' or '`>>>>>>>`' brackets appear somewhere other than the start of a line because they are appended to the incomplete line.

Without '`-m`', if an `ed` script option is specified and an incomplete line is found, `diff3` generates a warning and acts as if a newline had been present.

8.5 Saving the Changed File

Traditional Unix `diff3` generates an `ed` script without the trailing '`w`' and '`q`' commands that save the changes. System V `diff3` generates these extra commands. GNU `diff3` normally behaves like traditional Unix `diff3`, but with the '`-i`' option it behaves like System V `diff3` and appends the '`w`' and '`q`' commands.

The '`-i`' option requires one of the `ed` script options '`-AeExX3`', and is incompatible with the merged output option '`-m`'.

9 Interactive Merging with `sdiff`

With `sdiff`, you can merge two files interactively based on a side-by-side '`-y`' format comparison (see Section 2.3 [Side by Side], page 15). Use '`--output=file`' ('`-o file`') to specify where to put the merged text. See Chapter 16 [Invoking sdiff], page 73, for more details on the options to `sdiff`.

Another way to merge files interactively is to use the Emacs Lisp package `emerge`. See Section "emerge" in *The GNU Emacs Manual*, for more information.

9.1 Specifying `diff` Options to `sdiff`

The following `sdiff` options have the same meaning as for `diff`. See Section 13.1 [diff Options], page 61, for the use of these options.

```
-a -b -d -i -t -v
-B -E -I regexp -Z

--expand-tabs
--ignore-blank-lines  --ignore-case
--ignore-matching-lines=regexp  --ignore-space-change
--ignore-tab-expansion  --ignore-trailing-space
--left-column  --minimal  --speed-large-files
--strip-trailing-cr  --suppress-common-lines
--tabsize=columns  --text  --version  --width=columns
```

For historical reasons, `sdiff` has alternate names for some options. The '`-l`' option is equivalent to the '`--left-column`' option, and similarly '`-s`' is equivalent to '`--suppress-common-lines`'. The meaning of the `sdiff` '`-w`' and '`-W`' options is interchanged from that of `diff`: with `sdiff`, '`-w columns`' is equivalent to '`--width=columns`', and '`-W`' is equivalent to '`--ignore-all-space`'. `sdiff` without the '`-o`' option is equivalent to `diff` with the '`--side-by-side`' ('`-y`') option (see Section 2.3 [Side by Side], page 15).

9.2 Merge Commands

Groups of common lines, with a blank gutter, are copied from the first file to the output. After each group of differing lines, `sdiff` prompts with '`%`' and pauses, waiting for one of the following commands. Follow each command with RET.

'e'   Discard both versions. Invoke a text editor on an empty temporary file, then copy the resulting file to the output.

'eb'   Concatenate the two versions, edit the result in a temporary file, then copy the edited result to the output.

'ed'   Like 'eb', except precede each version with a header that shows what file and lines the version came from.

'el'
'e1'   Edit a copy of the left version, then copy the result to the output.

'er'
'e2'   Edit a copy of the right version, then copy the result to the output.

'l'
'1'   Copy the left version to the output.

'q'   Quit.

'r'
'2'   Copy the right version to the output.

's'   Silently copy common lines.

'v'   Verbosely copy common lines. This is the default.

The text editor invoked is specified by the **EDITOR** environment variable if it is set. The default is system-dependent.

10 Merging with `patch`

`patch` takes comparison output produced by `diff` and applies the differences to a copy of the original file, producing a patched version. With `patch`, you can distribute just the changes to a set of files instead of distributing the entire file set; your correspondents can apply `patch` to update their copy of the files with your changes. `patch` automatically determines the diff format, skips any leading or trailing headers, and uses the headers to determine which file to patch. This lets your correspondents feed a mail message containing a difference listing directly to `patch`.

`patch` detects and warns about common problems like forward patches. It saves any patches that it could not apply. It can also maintain a `patchlevel.h` file to ensure that your correspondents apply diffs in the proper order.

`patch` accepts a series of diffs in its standard input, usually separated by headers that specify which file to patch. It applies `diff` hunks (see Section 1.1 [Hunks], page 3) one by one. If a hunk does not exactly match the original file, `patch` uses heuristics to try to patch the file as well as it can. If no approximate match can be found, `patch` rejects the hunk and skips to the next hunk. `patch` normally replaces each file *f* with its new version, putting reject hunks (if any) into '`f.rej`'.

See Chapter 15 [Invoking patch], page 69, for detailed information on the options to `patch`.

10.1 Selecting the `patch` Input Format

`patch` normally determines which `diff` format the patch file uses by examining its contents. For patch files that contain particularly confusing leading text, you might need to use one of the following options to force `patch` to interpret the patch file as a certain format of diff. The output formats listed here are the only ones that `patch` can understand.

'`-c`'
'`--context`'
        context diff.

'`-e`'
'`--ed`'   ed script.

'`-n`'
'`--normal`'
        normal diff.

'`-u`'
'`--unified`'
        unified diff.

10.2 Revision Control

If a nonexistent input file is under a revision control system supported by `patch`, `patch` normally asks the user whether to get (or check out) the file from the revision control system. Patch currently supports RCS, ClearCase and SCCS. Under RCS and SCCS, `patch` also asks when the input file is read-only and matches the default version in the revision control system.

The '--get=num' ('-g num') option affects access to files under supported revision control systems. If num is positive, patch gets the file without asking the user; if zero, patch neither asks the user nor gets the file; and if negative, patch asks the user before getting the file. The default value of num is given by the value of the PATCH_GET environment variable if it is set; if not, the default value is zero if patch is conforming to POSIX, negative otherwise. See Section 10.12 [patch and POSIX], page 53.

The choice of revision control system is unaffected by the VERSION_CONTROL environment variable (see Section 10.9 [Backup Names], page 50).

10.3 Applying Imperfect Patches

patch tries to skip any leading text in the patch file, apply the diff, and then skip any trailing text. Thus you can feed a mail message directly to patch, and it should work. If the entire diff is indented by a constant amount of white space, patch automatically ignores the indentation. If a context diff contains trailing carriage return on each line, patch automatically ignores the carriage return. If a context diff has been encapsulated by prepending '- ' to lines beginning with '-' as per Internet RFC 934, patch automatically unencapsulates the input.

However, certain other types of imperfect input require user intervention or testing.

10.3.1 Applying Patches with Changed White Space

Sometimes mailers, editors, or other programs change spaces into tabs, or vice versa. If this happens to a patch file or an input file, the files might look the same, but patch will not be able to match them properly. If this problem occurs, use the '-l' or '--ignore-white-space' option, which makes patch compare blank characters (i.e. spaces and tabs) loosely so that any nonempty sequence of blanks in the patch file matches any nonempty sequence of blanks in the input files. Non-blank characters must still match exactly. Each line of the context must still match a line in the input file.

10.3.2 Applying Reversed Patches

Sometimes people run diff with the new file first instead of second. This creates a diff that is "reversed". To apply such patches, give patch the '--reverse' ('-R') option. patch then attempts to swap each hunk around before applying it. Rejects come out in the swapped format.

Often patch can guess that the patch is reversed. If the first hunk of a patch fails, patch reverses the hunk to see if it can apply it that way. If it can, patch asks you if you want to have the '-R' option set; if it can't, patch continues to apply the patch normally. This method cannot detect a reversed patch if it is a normal diff and the first command is an append (which should have been a delete) since appends always succeed, because a null context matches anywhere. But most patches add or change lines rather than delete them, so most reversed normal diffs begin with a delete, which fails, and patch notices.

If you apply a patch that you have already applied, patch thinks it is a reversed patch and offers to un-apply the patch. This could be construed as a feature. If you did this inadvertently and you don't want to un-apply the patch, just answer 'n' to this offer and to the subsequent "apply anyway" question—or type C-c to kill the patch process.

10.3.3 Helping `patch` Find Inexact Matches

For context diffs, and to a lesser extent normal diffs, `patch` can detect when the line numbers mentioned in the patch are incorrect, and it attempts to find the correct place to apply each hunk of the patch. As a first guess, it takes the line number mentioned in the hunk, plus or minus any offset used in applying the previous hunk. If that is not the correct place, `patch` scans both forward and backward for a set of lines matching the context given in the hunk.

First `patch` looks for a place where all lines of the context match. If it cannot find such a place, and it is reading a context or unified diff, and the maximum fuzz factor is set to 1 or more, then `patch` makes another scan, ignoring the first and last line of context. If that fails, and the maximum fuzz factor is set to 2 or more, it makes another scan, ignoring the first two and last two lines of context are ignored. It continues similarly if the maximum fuzz factor is larger.

The '`--fuzz=lines`' ('`-F lines`') option sets the maximum fuzz factor to *lines*. This option only applies to context and unified diffs; it ignores up to *lines* lines while looking for the place to install a hunk. Note that a larger fuzz factor increases the odds of making a faulty patch. The default fuzz factor is 2; there is no point to setting it to more than the number of lines of context in the diff, ordinarily 3.

If `patch` cannot find a place to install a hunk of the patch, it writes the hunk out to a reject file (see Section 10.10 [Reject Names], page 51, for information on how reject files are named). It writes out rejected hunks in context format no matter what form the input patch is in. If the input is a normal or `ed` diff, many of the contexts are simply null. The line numbers on the hunks in the reject file may be different from those in the patch file: they show the approximate location where `patch` thinks the failed hunks belong in the new file rather than in the old one.

If the '`--verbose`' option is given, then as it completes each hunk `patch` tells you whether the hunk succeeded or failed, and if it failed, on which line (in the new file) `patch` thinks the hunk should go. If this is different from the line number specified in the diff, it tells you the offset. A single large offset *may* indicate that `patch` installed a hunk in the wrong place. `patch` also tells you if it used a fuzz factor to make the match, in which case you should also be slightly suspicious.

`patch` cannot tell if the line numbers are off in an `ed` script, and can only detect wrong line numbers in a normal diff when it finds a change or delete command. It may have the same problem with a context diff using a fuzz factor equal to or greater than the number of lines of context shown in the diff (typically 3). In these cases, you should probably look at a context diff between your original and patched input files to see if the changes make sense. Compiling without errors is a pretty good indication that the patch worked, but not a guarantee.

A patch against an empty file applies to a nonexistent file, and vice versa. See Section 10.4 [Creating and Removing], page 48.

`patch` usually produces the correct results, even when it must make many guesses. However, the results are guaranteed only when the patch is applied to an exact copy of the file that the patch was generated from.

10.3.4 Predicting what `patch` will do

It may not be obvious in advance what `patch` will do with a complicated or poorly formatted patch. If you are concerned that the input might cause `patch` to modify the wrong files, you can use the '`--dry-run`' option, which causes `patch` to print the results of applying patches without actually changing any files. You can then inspect the diagnostics generated by the dry run to see whether `patch` will modify the files that you expect. If the patch does not do what you want, you can modify the patch (or the other options to `patch`) and try another dry run. Once you are satisfied with the proposed patch you can apply it by invoking `patch` as before, but this time without the '`--dry-run`' option.

10.4 Creating and Removing Files

Sometimes when comparing two directories, a file may exist in one directory but not the other. If you give `diff` the '`--new-file`' ('`-N`') option, or if you supply an old or new file that is named '`/dev/null`' or is empty and is dated the Epoch (1970-01-01 00:00:00 UTC), `diff` outputs a patch that adds or deletes the contents of this file. When given such a patch, `patch` normally creates a new file or removes the old file. However, when conforming to POSIX (see Section 10.12 [patch and POSIX], page 53), `patch` does not remove the old file, but leaves it empty. The '`--remove-empty-files`' ('`-E`') option causes `patch` to remove output files that are empty after applying a patch, even if the patch does not appear to be one that removed the file.

If the patch appears to create a file that already exists, `patch` asks for confirmation before applying the patch.

10.5 Updating Time Stamps on Patched Files

When `patch` updates a file, it normally sets the file's last-modified time stamp to the current time of day. If you are using `patch` to track a software distribution, this can cause `make` to incorrectly conclude that a patched file is out of date. For example, if '`syntax.c`' depends on '`syntax.y`', and `patch` updates '`syntax.c`' and then '`syntax.y`', then '`syntax.c`' will normally appear to be out of date with respect to '`syntax.y`' even though its contents are actually up to date.

The '`--set-utc`' ('`-Z`') option causes `patch` to set a patched file's modification and access times to the time stamps given in context diff headers. If the context diff headers do not specify a time zone, they are assumed to use Coordinated Universal Time (UTC, often known as GMT).

The '`--set-time`' ('`-T`') option acts like '`-Z`' or '`--set-utc`', except that it assumes that the context diff headers' time stamps use local time instead of UTC. This option is not recommended, because patches using local time cannot easily be used by people in other time zones, and because local time stamps are ambiguous when local clocks move backwards during daylight-saving time adjustments. If the context diff headers specify a time zone, this option is equivalent to '`--set-utc`' ('`-Z`').

`patch` normally refrains from setting a file's time stamps if the file's original last-modified time stamp does not match the time given in the diff header, of if the file's contents do not exactly match the patch. However, if the '`--force`' ('`-f`') option is given, the file's time stamps are set regardless.

Due to the limitations of the current `diff` format, `patch` cannot update the times of files whose contents have not changed. Also, if you set file time stamps to values other than the current time of day, you should also remove (e.g., with '`make clean`') all files that depend on the patched files, so that later invocations of `make` do not get confused by the patched files' times.

10.6 Multiple Patches in a File

If the patch file contains more than one patch, and if you do not specify an input file on the command line, `patch` tries to apply each patch as if they came from separate patch files. This means that it determines the name of the file to patch for each patch, and that it examines the leading text before each patch for file names and prerequisite revision level (see Chapter 11 [Making Patches], page 55, for more on that topic).

`patch` uses the following rules to intuit a file name from the leading text before a patch. First, `patch` takes an ordered list of candidate file names as follows:

- If the header is that of a context diff, `patch` takes the old and new file names in the header. A name is ignored if it does not have enough slashes to satisfy the '`-pnum`' or '`--strip=num`' option. The name '`/dev/null`' is also ignored.

- If there is an '`Index:`' line in the leading garbage and if either the old and new names are both absent or if `patch` is conforming to POSIX, `patch` takes the name in the '`Index:`' line.

- For the purpose of the following rules, the candidate file names are considered to be in the order (old, new, index), regardless of the order that they appear in the header.

Then `patch` selects a file name from the candidate list as follows:

- If some of the named files exist, `patch` selects the first name if conforming to POSIX, and the best name otherwise.

- If `patch` is not ignoring RCS, ClearCase, and SCCS (see Section 10.2 [Revision Control], page 45), and no named files exist but an RCS, ClearCase, or SCCS master is found, `patch` selects the first named file with an RCS, ClearCase, or SCCS master.

- If no named files exist, no RCS, ClearCase, or SCCS master was found, some names are given, `patch` is not conforming to POSIX, and the patch appears to create a file, `patch` selects the best name requiring the creation of the fewest directories.

- If no file name results from the above heuristics, you are asked for the name of the file to patch, and `patch` selects that name.

To determine the *best* of a nonempty list of file names, `patch` first takes all the names with the fewest path name components; of those, it then takes all the names with the shortest basename; of those, it then takes all the shortest names; finally, it takes the first remaining name.

See Section 10.12 [patch and POSIX], page 53, to see whether `patch` is conforming to POSIX.

10.7 Applying Patches in Other Directories

The '`--directory=directory`' ('`-d directory`') option to `patch` makes directory *directory* the current directory for interpreting both file names in the patch file, and file names given as arguments to other options (such as '-B' and '-o'). For example, while in a mail reading program, you can patch a file in the '/usr/src/emacs' directory directly from a message containing the patch like this:

```
| patch -d /usr/src/emacs
```

Sometimes the file names given in a patch contain leading directories, but you keep your files in a directory different from the one given in the patch. In those cases, you can use the '--strip=number' ('-pnumber') option to set the file name strip count to number. The strip count tells patch how many slashes, along with the directory names between them, to strip from the front of file names. A sequence of one or more adjacent slashes is counted as a single slash. By default, patch strips off all leading directories, leaving just the base file names.

For example, suppose the file name in the patch file is '/gnu/src/emacs/etc/NEWS'. Using '-p0' gives the entire file name unmodified, '-p1' gives 'gnu/src/emacs/etc/NEWS' (no leading slash), '-p4' gives 'etc/NEWS', and not specifying '-p' at all gives 'NEWS'.

patch looks for each file (after any slashes have been stripped) in the current directory, or if you used the '-d directory' option, in that directory.

10.8 Backup Files

Normally, patch creates a backup file if the patch does not exactly match the original input file, because in that case the original data might not be recovered if you undo the patch with 'patch -R' (see Section 10.3.2 [Reversed Patches], page 46). However, when conforming to POSIX, patch does not create backup files by default. See Section 10.12 [patch and POSIX], page 53.

The '--backup' ('-b') option causes patch to make a backup file regardless of whether the patch matches the original input. The '--backup-if-mismatch' option causes patch to create backup files for mismatches files; this is the default when not conforming to POSIX. The '--no-backup-if-mismatch' option causes patch to not create backup files, even for mismatched patches; this is the default when conforming to POSIX.

When backing up a file that does not exist, an empty, unreadable backup file is created as a placeholder to represent the nonexistent file.

10.9 Backup File Names

Normally, patch renames an original input file into a backup file by appending to its name the extension '.orig', or '~' if using '.orig' would make the backup file name too long.[1] The '-z backup-suffix' or '--suffix=backup-suffix' option causes patch to use backup-suffix as the backup extension instead.

Alternately, you can specify the extension for backup files with the SIMPLE_BACKUP_SUFFIX environment variable, which the options override.

patch can also create numbered backup files the way GNU Emacs does. With this method, instead of having a single backup of each file, patch makes a new backup file name each time it patches a file. For example, the backups of a file named 'sink' would be called, successively, 'sink.~1~', 'sink.~2~', 'sink.~3~', etc.

---

[1] A coding error in GNU patch version 2.5.4 causes it to always use '~', but this should be fixed in the next release.

The '`-V backup-style`' or '`--version-control=backup-style`' option takes as an argument a method for creating backup file names. You can alternately control the type of backups that `patch` makes with the `PATCH_VERSION_CONTROL` environment variable, which the '`-V`' option overrides. If `PATCH_VERSION_CONTROL` is not set, the `VERSION_CONTROL` environment variable is used instead. Please note that these options and variables control backup file names; they do not affect the choice of revision control system (see Section 10.2 [Revision Control], page 45).

The values of these environment variables and the argument to the '`-V`' option are like the GNU Emacs `version-control` variable (see Section "Backup Names" in *The GNU Emacs Manual*, for more information on backup versions in Emacs). They also recognize synonyms that are more descriptive. The valid values are listed below; unique abbreviations are acceptable.

'`t`'
'`numbered`'
> Always make numbered backups.

'`nil`'
'`existing`'
> Make numbered backups of files that already have them, simple backups of the others. This is the default.

'`never`'
'`simple`'   Always make simple backups.

You can also tell `patch` to prepend a prefix, such as a directory name, to produce backup file names. The '`--prefix=prefix`' ('`-B prefix`') option makes backup files by prepending *prefix* to them. The '`--basename-prefix=prefix`' ('`-Y prefix`') prepends *prefix* to the last file name component of backup file names instead; for example, '`-Y ~`' causes the backup name for '`dir/file.c`' to be '`dir/~file.c`'. If you use either of these prefix options, the suffix-based options are ignored.

If you specify the output file with the '`-o`' option, that file is the one that is backed up, not the input file.

Options that affect the names of backup files do not affect whether backups are made. For example, if you specify the '`--no-backup-if-mismatch`' option, none of the options described in this section have any affect, because no backups are made.

10.10 Reject File Names

The names for reject files (files containing patches that `patch` could not find a place to apply) are normally the name of the output file with '`.rej`' appended (or '`#`' if using '`.rej`' would make the backup file name too long).

Alternatively, you can tell `patch` to place all of the rejected patches in a single file. The '`-r reject-file`' or '`--reject-file=reject-file`' option uses *reject-file* as the reject file name.

10.11 Messages and Questions from `patch`

`patch` can produce a variety of messages, especially if it has trouble decoding its input. In a few situations where it's not sure how to proceed, `patch` normally prompts you for more information from the keyboard. There are options to produce more or fewer messages, to have it not ask for keyboard input, and to affect the way that file names are quoted in messages.

`patch` exits with status 0 if all hunks are applied successfully, 1 if some hunks cannot be applied, and 2 if there is more serious trouble. When applying a set of patches in a loop, you should check the exit status, so you don't apply a later patch to a partially patched file.

10.11.1 Controlling the Verbosity of `patch`

You can cause `patch` to produce more messages by using the '`--verbose`' option. For example, when you give this option, the message '`Hmm...`' indicates that `patch` is reading text in the patch file, attempting to determine whether there is a patch in that text, and if so, what kind of patch it is.

You can inhibit all terminal output from `patch`, unless an error occurs, by using the '`-s`', '`--quiet`', or '`--silent`' option.

10.11.2 Inhibiting Keyboard Input

There are two ways you can prevent `patch` from asking you any questions. The '`--force`' ('`-f`') option assumes that you know what you are doing. It causes `patch` to do the following:

- Skip patches that do not contain file names in their headers.
- Patch files even though they have the wrong version for the '`Prereq:`' line in the patch;
- Assume that patches are not reversed even if they look like they are.

The '`--batch`' ('`-t`') option is similar to '`-f`', in that it suppresses questions, but it makes somewhat different assumptions:

- Skip patches that do not contain file names in their headers (the same as '`-f`').
- Skip patches for which the file has the wrong version for the '`Prereq:`' line in the patch;
- Assume that patches are reversed if they look like they are.

10.11.3 `patch` Quoting Style

When `patch` outputs a file name in a diagnostic message, it can format the name in any of several ways. This can be useful to output file names unambiguously, even if they contain punctuation or special characters like newlines. The '`--quoting-style=word`' option controls how names are output. The *word* should be one of the following:

'`literal`' Output names as-is.

'`shell`' Quote names for the shell if they contain shell metacharacters or would cause ambiguous output.

'`shell-always`'
           Quote names for the shell, even if they would normally not require quoting.

'`c`'   Quote names as for a C language string.

'`escape`' Quote as with '`c`' except omit the surrounding double-quote characters.

You can specify the default value of the '`--quoting-style`' option with the environment variable `QUOTING_STYLE`. If that environment variable is not set, the default value is '`shell`', but this default may change in a future version of `patch`.

10.12 `patch` and the POSIX Standard

If you specify the '`--posix`' option, or set the `POSIXLY_CORRECT` environment variable, `patch` conforms more strictly to the POSIX standard, as follows:

- Take the first existing file from the list (old, new, index) when intuiting file names from diff headers. See Section 10.6 [Multiple Patches], page 49.

- Do not remove files that are removed by a diff. See Section 10.4 [Creating and Removing], page 48.

- Do not ask whether to get files from RCS, ClearCase, or SCCS. See Section 10.2 [Revision Control], page 45.

- Require that all options precede the files in the command line.

- Do not backup files, even when there is a mismatch. See Section 10.8 [Backups], page 50.

10.13 GNU `patch` and Traditional `patch`

The current version of GNU `patch` normally follows the POSIX standard. See Section 10.12 [patch and POSIX], page 53, for the few exceptions to this general rule.

Unfortunately, POSIX redefined the behavior of `patch` in several important ways. You should be aware of the following differences if you must interoperate with traditional `patch`, or with GNU `patch` version 2.1 and earlier.

- In traditional `patch`, the '`-p`' option's operand was optional, and a bare '`-p`' was equivalent to '`-p0`'. The '`-p`' option now requires an operand, and '`-p 0`' is now equivalent to '`-p0`'. For maximum compatibility, use options like '`-p0`' and '`-p1`'.

  Also, traditional `patch` simply counted slashes when stripping path prefixes; `patch` now counts pathname components. That is, a sequence of one or more adjacent slashes now counts as a single slash. For maximum portability, avoid sending patches containing '`//`' in file names.

- In traditional `patch`, backups were enabled by default. This behavior is now enabled with the '`--backup`' ('`-b`') option.

  Conversely, in POSIX `patch`, backups are never made, even when there is a mismatch. In GNU `patch`, this behavior is enabled with the '`--no-backup-if-mismatch`' option, or by conforming to POSIX.

  The '`-b `*`suffix`*'' option of traditional `patch` is equivalent to the '`-b -z `*`suffix`*'' options of GNU `patch`.

- Traditional `patch` used a complicated (and incompletely documented) method to intuit the name of the file to be patched from the patch header. This method did not conform to POSIX, and had a few gotchas. Now `patch` uses a different, equally complicated (but better documented) method that is optionally POSIX-conforming; we hope it has fewer gotchas. The two methods are compatible if the file names in the context diff header and the '`Index:`' line are all identical after prefix-stripping. Your patch is normally compatible if each header's file names all contain the same number of slashes.

- When traditional `patch` asked the user a question, it sent the question to standard error and looked for an answer from the first file in the following list that was a terminal: standard error, standard output, '`/dev/tty`', and standard input. Now `patch` sends questions to standard output and gets answers from '/dev/tty'. Defaults for some answers have been changed so that patch never goes into an infinite loop when using default answers.

- Traditional patch exited with a status value that counted the number of bad hunks, or with status 1 if there was real trouble. Now patch exits with status 1 if some hunks failed, or with 2 if there was real trouble.

- Limit yourself to the following options when sending instructions meant to be executed by anyone running GNU patch, traditional patch, or a patch that conforms to POSIX. Spaces are significant in the following list, and operands are required.

  '-c'
  '-d *dir*'
  '-D *define*'
  '-e'
  '-l'
  '-n'
  '-N'
  '-o *outfile*'
  '-*pnum*'
  '-R'
  '-r *rejectfile*'

11 Tips for Making and Using Patches

Use some common sense when making and using patches. For example, when sending bug fixes to a program's maintainer, send several small patches, one per independent subject, instead of one large, harder-to-digest patch that covers all the subjects.

Here are some other things you should keep in mind if you are going to distribute patches for updating a software package.

11.1 Tips for Patch Producers

To create a patch that changes an older version of a package into a newer version, first make a copy of the older and newer versions in adjacent subdirectories. It is common to do that by unpacking `tar` archives of the two versions.

To generate the patch, use the command '`diff -Naur old new`' where *old* and *new* identify the old and new directories. The names *old* and *new* should not contain any slashes. The '`-N`' option lets the patch create and remove files; '`-a`' lets the patch update non-text files; '`-u`' generates useful time stamps and enough context; and '`-r`' lets the patch update subdirectories. Here is an example command, using Bourne shell syntax:

```
diff -Naur gcc-3.0.3 gcc-3.0.4
```

Tell your recipients how to apply the patches. This should include which working directory to use, and which `patch` options to use; the option '`-p1`' is recommended. Test your procedure by pretending to be a recipient and applying your patches to a copy of the original files.

See Section 11.3 [Avoiding Common Mistakes], page 55, for how to avoid common mistakes when generating a patch.

11.2 Tips for Patch Consumers

A patch producer should tell recipients how to apply the patches, so the first rule of thumb for a patch consumer is to follow the instructions supplied with the patch.

GNU `diff` can analyze files with arbitrarily long lines and files that end in incomplete lines. However, older versions of `patch` cannot patch such files. If you are having trouble applying such patches, try upgrading to a recent version of GNU `patch`.

11.3 Avoiding Common Mistakes

When producing a patch for multiple files, apply `diff` to directories whose names do not have slashes. This reduces confusion when the patch consumer specifies the '`-pnumber`' option, since this option can have surprising results when the old and new file names have different numbers of slashes. For example, do not send a patch with a header that looks like this:

```
diff -Naur v2.0.29/prog/README prog/README
--- v2.0.29/prog/README 2002-03-10 23:30:39.942229878 -0800
+++ prog/README 2002-03-17 20:49:32.442260588 -0800
```

because the two file names have different numbers of slashes, and different versions of `patch` interpret the file names differently. To avoid confusion, send output that looks like this instead:

```
diff -Naur v2.0.29/prog/README v2.0.30/prog/README
--- v2.0.29/prog/README 2002-03-10 23:30:39.942229878 -0800
+++ v2.0.30/prog/README 2002-03-17 20:49:32.442260588 -0800
```

Make sure you have specified the file names correctly, either in a context diff header or with an 'Index:' line. Take care to not send out reversed patches, since these make people wonder whether they have already applied the patch.

Avoid sending patches that compare backup file names like 'README.orig' or 'README~', since this might confuse patch into patching a backup file instead of the real file. Instead, send patches that compare the same base file names in different directories, e.g. 'old/README' and 'new/README'.

To save people from partially applying a patch before other patches that should have gone before it, you can make the first patch in the patch file update a file with a name like 'patchlevel.h' or 'version.c', which contains a patch level or version number. If the input file contains the wrong version number, patch will complain immediately.

An even clearer way to prevent this problem is to put a 'Prereq:' line before the patch. If the leading text in the patch file contains a line that starts with 'Prereq:', patch takes the next word from that line (normally a version number) and checks whether the next input file contains that word, preceded and followed by either white space or a newline. If not, patch prompts you for confirmation before proceeding. This makes it difficult to accidentally apply patches in the wrong order.

11.4 Generating Smaller Patches

The simplest way to generate a patch is to use 'diff -Naur' (see Section 11.1 [Tips for Patch Producers], page 55), but you might be able to reduce the size of the patch by renaming or removing some files before making the patch. If the older version of the package contains any files that the newer version does not, or if any files have been renamed between the two versions, make a list of rm and mv commands for the user to execute in the old version directory before applying the patch. Then run those commands yourself in the scratch directory.

If there are any files that you don't need to include in the patch because they can easily be rebuilt from other files (for example, 'TAGS' and output from yacc and makeinfo), exclude them from the patch by giving diff the '-x pattern' option (see Chapter 4 [Comparing Directories], page 29). If you want your patch to modify a derived file because your recipients lack tools to build it, make sure that the patch for the derived file follows any patches for files that it depends on, so that the recipients' time stamps will not confuse make.

Now you can create the patch using 'diff -Naur'. Make sure to specify the scratch directory first and the newer directory second.

Add to the top of the patch a note telling the user any rm and mv commands to run before applying the patch. Then you can remove the scratch directory.

You can also shrink the patch size by using fewer lines of context, but bear in mind that patch typically needs at least two lines for proper operation when patches do not exactly match the input files.

12 Invoking cmp

The cmp command compares two files, and if they differ, tells the first byte and line number where they differ or reports that one file is a prefix of the other. Bytes and lines are numbered starting with 1. The arguments of cmp are as follows:

> cmp *options*... *from-file* [*to-file* [*from-skip* [*to-skip*]]]

The file name '-' is always the standard input. cmp also uses the standard input if one file name is omitted. The *from-skip* and *to-skip* operands specify how many bytes to ignore at the start of each file; they are equivalent to the '--ignore-initial=*from-skip*:*to-skip*' option.

By default, cmp outputs nothing if the two files have the same contents. If one file is a prefix of the other, cmp prints to standard error a message of the following form:

> cmp: EOF on *shorter-file*

Otherwise, cmp prints to standard output a message of the following form:

> *from-file* *to-file* differ: char *byte-number*, line *line-number*

The message formats can differ outside the POSIX locale. Also, POSIX allows the EOF message to be followed by a blank and some additional information.

An exit status of 0 means no differences were found, 1 means some differences were found, and 2 means trouble.

12.1 Options to cmp

Below is a summary of all of the options that GNU cmp accepts. Most options have two equivalent names, one of which is a single letter preceded by '-', and the other of which is a long name preceded by '--'. Multiple single letter options (unless they take an argument) can be combined into a single command line word: '-bl' is equivalent to '-b -l'.

'-b'
'--print-bytes'

> Print the differing bytes. Display control bytes as a '^' followed by a letter of the alphabet and precede bytes that have the high bit set with 'M-' (which stands for "meta").

'--help'   Output a summary of usage and then exit.

'-i *skip*'
'--ignore-initial=*skip*'

> Ignore any differences in the first *skip* bytes of the input files. Treat files with fewer than *skip* bytes as if they are empty. If *skip* is of the form '*from-skip*:*to-skip*', skip the first *from-skip* bytes of the first input file and the first *to-skip* bytes of the second.

'-l'
'--verbose'

> Output the (decimal) byte numbers and (octal) values of all differing bytes, instead of the default standard output. Each output line contains a differing byte's number relative to the start of the input, followed by the differing byte values. Byte numbers start at 1. Also, output the EOF message if one file is shorter than the other.

'`-n count`'
'`--bytes=count`'
> Compare at most *count* input bytes.

'`-s`'
'`--quiet`'
'`--silent`'
> Do not print anything; only return an exit status indicating whether the files differ.

'`-v`'
'`--version`'
> Output version information and then exit.

In the above table, operands that are byte counts are normally decimal, but may be preceded by '`0`' for octal and '`0x`' for hexadecimal.

A byte count can be followed by a suffix to specify a multiple of that count; in this case an omitted integer is understood to be 1. A bare size letter, or one followed by '`iB`', specifies a multiple using powers of 1024. A size letter followed by '`B`' specifies powers of 1000 instead. For example, '`-n 4M`' and '`-n 4MiB`' are equivalent to '`-n 4194304`', whereas '`-n 4MB`' is equivalent to '`-n 4000000`'. This notation is upward compatible with the SI prefixes for decimal multiples and with the IEC 60027-2 prefixes for binary multiples.

The following suffixes are defined. Large sizes like `1Y` may be rejected by your computer due to limitations of its arithmetic.

'`kB`'   kilobyte: $10^3 = 1000$.

'`k`'
'`K`'
'`KiB`'   kibibyte: $2^10 = 1024$. '`K`' is special: the SI prefix is '`k`' and the IEC 60027-2 prefix is '`Ki`', but tradition and POSIX use '`k`' to mean '`KiB`'.

'`MB`'   megabyte: $10^6 = 1,000,000$.

'`M`'
'`MiB`'   mebibyte: $2^20 = 1,048,576$.

'`GB`'   gigabyte: $10^9 = 1,000,000,000$.

'`G`'
'`GiB`'   gibibyte: $2^30 = 1,073,741,824$.

'`TB`'   terabyte: $10^12 = 1,000,000,000,000$.

'`T`'
'`TiB`'   tebibyte: $2^40 = 1,099,511,627,776$.

'`PB`'   petabyte: $10^15 = 1,000,000,000,000,000$.

'`P`'
'`PiB`'   pebibyte: $2^50 = 1,125,899,906,842,624$.

'`EB`'   exabyte: $10^18 = 1,000,000,000,000,000,000$.

'E'
'EiB'   exbibyte: $2^60 = 1,152,921,504,606,846,976.$

'ZB'   zettabyte: $10^21 = 1,000,000,000,000,000,000,000$

'Z'
'ZiB' $2^70 = 1,180,591,620,717,411,303,424.$ ('Zi' is a GNU extension to IEC 60027-
              2.)

'YB'   yottabyte: $10^24 = 1,000,000,000,000,000,000,000,000.$

'Y'
'YiB' $2^80 = 1,208,925,819,614,629,174,706,176.$ ('Yi' is a GNU extension to IEC
              60027-2.)

13 Invoking `diff`

The format for running the `diff` command is:

    diff *options... files...*

In the simplest case, two file names *from-file* and *to-file* are given, and `diff` compares the contents of *from-file* and *to-file*. A file name of '-' stands for text read from the standard input. As a special case, '`diff - -`' compares a copy of standard input to itself.

If one file is a directory and the other is not, `diff` compares the file in the directory whose name is that of the non-directory. The non-directory file must not be '-'.

If two file names are given and both are directories, `diff` compares corresponding files in both directories, in alphabetical order; this comparison is not recursive unless the '`--recursive`' ('`-r`') option is given. `diff` never compares the actual contents of a directory as if it were a file. The file that is fully specified may not be standard input, because standard input is nameless and the notion of "file with the same name" does not apply.

If the '`--from-file=file`' option is given, the number of file names is arbitrary, and *file* is compared to each named file. Similarly, if the '`--to-file=file`' option is given, each named file is compared to *file*.

`diff` options begin with '-', so normally file names may not begin with '-'. However, '`--`' as an argument by itself treats the remaining arguments as file names even if they begin with '-'.

An exit status of 0 means no differences were found, 1 means some differences were found, and 2 means trouble. Normally, differing binary files count as trouble, but this can be altered by using the '`--text`' ('`-a`') option, or the '`-q`' or '`--brief`' option.

13.1 Options to `diff`

Below is a summary of all of the options that GNU `diff` accepts. Most options have two equivalent names, one of which is a single letter preceded by '-', and the other of which is a long name preceded by '`--`'. Multiple single letter options (unless they take an argument) can be combined into a single command line word: '`-ac`' is equivalent to '`-a -c`'. Long named options can be abbreviated to any unique prefix of their name. Brackets ([and]) indicate that an option takes an optional argument.

'`-a`'
'`--text`'   Treat all files as text and compare them line-by-line, even if they do not seem to be text. See Section 1.7 [Binary], page 6.

'`-b`'
'`--ignore-space-change`'
                Ignore changes in amount of white space. See Section 1.2 [White Space], page 4.

'`-B`'
'`--ignore-blank-lines`'
                Ignore changes that just insert or delete blank lines. See Section 1.3 [Blank Lines], page 4.

'`--binary`'
                Read and write data in binary mode. See Section 1.7 [Binary], page 6.

'-c'   Use the context output format, showing three lines of context. See Section 2.2.1
                [Context Format], page 10.

'-C *lines*'
'--context[=*lines*]'
                Use the context output format, showing *lines* (an integer) lines of context, or
                three if *lines* is not given. See Section 2.2.1 [Context Format], page 10. For
                proper operation, patch typically needs at least two lines of context.

                For compatibility diff also supports an obsolete option syntax '-*lines*' that
                has effect when combined with '-c', '-p', or '-u'. New scripts should use '-U
                lines' ('-C *lines*') instead.

'--changed-group-format=*format*'
                Use *format* to output a line group containing differing lines from both files in
                if-then-else format. See Section 2.6.1 [Line Group Formats], page 20.

'-d'
'--minimal'
                Change the algorithm perhaps find a smaller set of changes. This makes diff
                slower (sometimes much slower). See Chapter 6 [diff Performance], page 33.

'-D *name*'
'--ifdef=*name*'
                Make merged '#ifdef' format output, conditional on the preprocessor macro
                name. See Section 2.6 [If-then-else], page 19.

'-e'
'--ed'   Make output that is a valid ed script. See Section 2.5.1 [ed Scripts], page 17.

'-E'
'--ignore-tab-expansion'
                Ignore changes due to tab expansion. See Section 1.2 [White Space], page 4.

'-f'
'--forward-ed'
                Make output that looks vaguely like an ed script but has changes in the order
                they appear in the file. See Section 2.5.2 [Forward ed], page 18.

'-F *regexp*'
'--show-function-line=*regexp*'
                In context and unified format, for each hunk of differences, show some of the last
                preceding line that matches *regexp*. See Section 2.2.3.1 [Specified Headings],
                page 14.

'--from-file=*file*'
                Compare *file* to each operand; *file* may be a directory.

'--help'   Output a summary of usage and then exit.

'--horizon-lines=*lines*'
                Do not discard the last *lines* lines of the common prefix and the first *lines* lines
                of the common suffix. See Chapter 6 [diff Performance], page 33.

'`-i`'
'`--ignore-case`'
>	Ignore changes in case; consider upper- and lower-case letters equivalent. See Section 1.5 [Case Folding], page 5.

'`-I regexp`'
'`--ignore-matching-lines=regexp`'
>	Ignore changes that just insert or delete lines that match *regexp*. See Section 1.4 [Specified Lines], page 5.

'`--ignore-file-name-case`'
>	Ignore case when comparing file names. For example, recursive comparison of '`d`' to '`e`' might compare the contents of '`d/Init`' and '`e/inIt`'. At the top level, '`diff d inIt`' might compare the contents of '`d/Init`' and '`inIt`'. See Chapter 4 [Comparing Directories], page 29.

'`-l`'
'`--paginate`'
>	Pass the output through `pr` to paginate it. See Section 5.3 [Pagination], page 31.

'`-L label`'
'`--label=label`'
>	Use *label* instead of the file name in the context format (see Section 2.2.1 [Context Format], page 10) and unified format (see Section 2.2.2 [Unified Format], page 12) headers. See Section 2.5.3 [RCS], page 19.

'`--left-column`'
>	Print only the left column of two common lines in side by side format. See Section 2.3.1 [Side by Side Format], page 15.

'`--line-format=format`'
>	Use *format* to output all input lines in if-then-else format. See Section 2.6.2 [Line Formats], page 22.

'`-n`'
'`--rcs`'	Output RCS-format diffs; like '`-f`' except that each command specifies the number of lines affected. See Section 2.5.3 [RCS], page 19.

'`-N`'
'`--new-file`'
>	If one file is missing, treat it as present but empty. See Chapter 4 [Comparing Directories], page 29.

'`--new-group-format=format`'
>	Use *format* to output a group of lines taken from just the second file in if-then-else format. See Section 2.6.1 [Line Group Formats], page 20.

'`--new-line-format=format`'
>	Use *format* to output a line taken from just the second file in if-then-else format. See Section 2.6.2 [Line Formats], page 22.

'`--no-dereference`'
>	Act on symbolic links themselves instead of what they point to.

'`--old-group-format=`*format*'

> Use *format* to output a group of lines taken from just the first file in if-then-else format. See Section 2.6.1 [Line Group Formats], page 20.

'`--old-line-format=`*format*'

> Use *format* to output a line taken from just the first file in if-then-else format. See Section 2.6.2 [Line Formats], page 22.

'`-p`'
'`--show-c-function`'

> Show which C function each change is in. See Section 2.2.3.2 [C Function Headings], page 14.

'`-q`'
'`--brief`' Report only whether the files differ, not the details of the differences. See Section 1.6 [Brief], page 5.

'`-r`'
'`--recursive`'

> When comparing directories, recursively compare any subdirectories found. See Chapter 4 [Comparing Directories], page 29.

'`-s`'
'`--report-identical-files`'

> Report when two files are the same. See Chapter 4 [Comparing Directories], page 29.

'`-S `*file*'
'`--starting-file=`*file*'

> When comparing directories, start with the file *file*. This is used for resuming an aborted comparison. See Chapter 4 [Comparing Directories], page 29.

'`--speed-large-files`'

> Use heuristics to speed handling of large files that have numerous scattered small changes. See Chapter 6 [diff Performance], page 33.

'`--strip-trailing-cr`'

> Strip any trailing carriage return at the end of an input line. See Section 1.7 [Binary], page 6.

'`--suppress-common-lines`'

> Do not print common lines in side by side format. See Section 2.3.1 [Side by Side Format], page 15.

'`-t`'
'`--expand-tabs`'

> Expand tabs to spaces in the output, to preserve the alignment of tabs in the input files. See Section 5.1 [Tabs], page 31.

'`-T`'
'`--initial-tab`'

> Output a tab rather than a space before the text of a line in normal or context format. This causes the alignment of tabs in the line to look normal. See Section 5.1 [Tabs], page 31.

'`--tabsize=columns`'

> Assume that tab stops are set every *columns* (default 8) print columns. See Section 5.1 [Tabs], page 31.

'`--suppress-blank-empty`'

> Suppress any blanks before newlines when printing the representation of an empty line, when outputting normal, context, or unified format. See Section 5.2 [Trailing Blanks], page 31.

'`--to-file=file`'

> Compare each operand to *file*; *file* may be a directory.

'`-u`'

> Use the unified output format, showing three lines of context. See Section 2.2.2 [Unified Format], page 12.

'`--unchanged-group-format=format`'

> Use *format* to output a group of common lines taken from both files in if-then-else format. See Section 2.6.1 [Line Group Formats], page 20.

'`--unchanged-line-format=format`'

> Use *format* to output a line common to both files in if-then-else format. See Section 2.6.2 [Line Formats], page 22.

'`--unidirectional-new-file`'

> If a first file is missing, treat it as present but empty. See Chapter 4 [Comparing Directories], page 29.

'`-U lines`'
'`--unified[=lines]`'

> Use the unified output format, showing *lines* (an integer) lines of context, or three if *lines* is not given. See Section 2.2.2 [Unified Format], page 12. For proper operation, `patch` typically needs at least two lines of context.

> On older systems, `diff` supports an obsolete option '`-lines`' that has effect when combined with '`-u`'. POSIX 1003.1-2001 (see Chapter 17 [Standards conformance], page 77) does not allow this; use '`-U lines`' instead.

'`-v`'
'`--version`'

> Output version information and then exit.

'`-w`'
'`--ignore-all-space`'

> Ignore white space when comparing lines. See Section 1.2 [White Space], page 4.

'`-W columns`'
'`--width=columns`'

> Output at most *columns* (default 130) print columns per line in side by side format. See Section 2.3.1 [Side by Side Format], page 15.

'`-x pattern`'
'`--exclude=pattern`'

> When comparing directories, ignore files and subdirectories whose basenames match *pattern*. See Chapter 4 [Comparing Directories], page 29.

'-X *file*'
'--exclude-from=*file*'

> When comparing directories, ignore files and subdirectories whose basenames match any pattern contained in *file*. See Chapter 4 [Comparing Directories], page 29.

'-y'
'--side-by-side'

> Use the side by side output format. See Section 2.3.1 [Side by Side Format], page 15.

'-Z'
'--ignore-trailing-space'

> Ignore white space at line end. See Section 1.2 [White Space], page 4.

14 Invoking `diff3`

The `diff3` command compares three files and outputs descriptions of their differences. Its arguments are as follows:

        diff3 *options... mine older yours*

The files to compare are *mine*, *older*, and *yours*. At most one of these three file names may be '-', which tells `diff3` to read the standard input for that file.

An exit status of 0 means `diff3` was successful, 1 means some conflicts were found, and 2 means trouble.

14.1 Options to `diff3`

Below is a summary of all of the options that GNU `diff3` accepts. Multiple single letter options (unless they take an argument) can be combined into a single command line argument.

'`-a`'
'`--text`'   Treat all files as text and compare them line-by-line, even if they do not appear to be text. See Section 1.7 [Binary], page 6.

'`-A`'
'`--show-all`'
            Incorporate all unmerged changes from *older* to *yours* into *mine*, surrounding conflicts with bracket lines. See Section 8.2 [Marking Conflicts], page 40.

'`--diff-program=`*program*'
            Use the compatible comparison program *program* to compare files instead of `diff`.

'`-e`'
'`--ed`'   Generate an `ed` script that incorporates all the changes from *older* to *yours* into *mine*. See Section 8.1 [Which Changes], page 39.

'`-E`'
'`--show-overlap`'
            Like '`-e`', except bracket lines from overlapping changes' first and third files. See Section 8.2 [Marking Conflicts], page 40. With '`-E`', an overlapping change looks like this:

                    <<<<<<< *mine*
                    lines from *mine*
                    =======
                    lines from *yours*
                    >>>>>>> *yours*

'`--help`'   Output a summary of usage and then exit.

'`-i`'   Generate '`w`' and '`q`' commands at the end of the `ed` script for System V compatibility. This option must be combined with one of the '`-AeExX3`' options, and may not be combined with '`-m`'. See Section 8.5 [Saving the Changed File], page 42.

'`--label=`*`label`*'

> Use the label *label* for the brackets output by the '`-A`', '`-E`' and '`-X`' options. This option may be given up to three times, one for each input file. The default labels are the names of the input files. Thus '`diff3 --label X --label Y --label Z -m A B C`' acts like '`diff3 -m A B C`', except that the output looks like it came from files named '`X`', '`Y`' and '`Z`' rather than from files named '`A`', '`B`' and '`C`'. See Section 8.2 [Marking Conflicts], page 40.

'`-m`'

'`--merge`' Apply the edit script to the first file and send the result to standard output. Unlike piping the output from `diff3` to `ed`, this works even for binary files and incomplete lines. '`-A`' is assumed if no edit script option is specified. See Section 8.3 [Bypassing ed], page 41.

'`--strip-trailing-cr`'

> Strip any trailing carriage return at the end of an input line. See Section 1.7 [Binary], page 6.

'`-T`'

'`--initial-tab`'

> Output a tab rather than two spaces before the text of a line in normal format. This causes the alignment of tabs in the line to look normal. See Section 5.1 [Tabs], page 31.

'`-v`'

'`--version`'

> Output version information and then exit.

'`-x`'

'`--overlap-only`'

> Like '`-e`', except output only the overlapping changes. See Section 8.1 [Which Changes], page 39.

'`-X`'   Like '`-E`', except output only the overlapping changes. In other words, like '`-x`', except bracket changes as in '`-E`'. See Section 8.2 [Marking Conflicts], page 40.

'`-3`'

'`--easy-only`'

> Like '`-e`', except output only the nonoverlapping changes. See Section 8.1 [Which Changes], page 39.

15 Invoking `patch`

Normally `patch` is invoked like this:

>   patch <patchfile

The full format for invoking `patch` is:

>   patch options... [origfile [patchfile]]

You can also specify where to read the patch from with the '-i *patchfile*' or '--input=*patchfile*' option. If you do not specify *patchfile*, or if *patchfile* is '-', `patch` reads the patch (that is, the `diff` output) from the standard input.

If you do not specify an input file on the command line, `patch` tries to intuit from the *leading text* (any text in the patch that comes before the `diff` output) which file to edit. See Section 10.6 [Multiple Patches], page 49.

By default, `patch` replaces the original input file with the patched version, possibly after renaming the original file into a backup file (see Section 10.9 [Backup Names], page 50, for a description of how `patch` names backup files). You can also specify where to put the output with the '-o *file*' or '--output=*file*' option; however, do not use this option if *file* is one of the input files.

15.1 Options to `patch`

Here is a summary of all of the options that GNU `patch` accepts. See Section 10.13 [patch and Tradition], page 53, for which of these options are safe to use in older versions of `patch`.

Multiple single-letter options that do not take an argument can be combined into a single command line argument with only one dash.

'-b'
'--backup'
>   Back up the original contents of each file, even if backups would normally not be made. See Section 10.8 [Backups], page 50.

'-B *prefix*'
'--prefix=*prefix*'
>   Prepend *prefix* to backup file names. See Section 10.9 [Backup Names], page 50.

'--backup-if-mismatch'
>   Back up the original contents of each file if the patch does not exactly match the file. This is the default behavior when not conforming to POSIX. See Section 10.8 [Backups], page 50.

'--binary'
>   Read and write all files in binary mode, except for standard output and '/dev/tty'. This option has no effect on POSIX-conforming systems like GNU/Linux. On systems where this option makes a difference, the patch should be generated by 'diff -a --binary'. See Section 1.7 [Binary], page 6.

'-c'
'--context'
>   Interpret the patch file as a context diff. See Section 10.1 [patch Input], page 45.

'-d *directory*'
'--directory=*directory*'

> Make directory *directory* the current directory for interpreting both file names in the patch file, and file names given as arguments to other options. See Section 10.7 [patch Directories], page 49.

'-D *name*'
'--ifdef=*name*'

> Make merged if-then-else output using *name*. See Section 2.6 [If-then-else], page 19.

'--dry-run'

> Print the results of applying the patches without actually changing any files. See Section 10.3.4 [Dry Runs], page 48.

'-e'
'--ed'   Interpret the patch file as an **ed** script. See Section 10.1 [patch Input], page 45.

'-E'
'--remove-empty-files'

> Remove output files that are empty after the patches have been applied. See Section 10.4 [Creating and Removing], page 48.

'-f'
'--force' Assume that the user knows exactly what he or she is doing, and do not ask any questions. See Section 10.11 [patch Messages], page 51.

'-F *lines*'
'--fuzz=*lines*'

> Set the maximum fuzz factor to *lines*. See Section 10.3.3 [Inexact], page 47.

'-g *num*'
'--get=*num*'

> If *num* is positive, get input files from a revision control system as necessary; if zero, do not get the files; if negative, ask the user whether to get the files. See Section 10.2 [Revision Control], page 45.

'--help'   Output a summary of usage and then exit.

'-i *patchfile*'
'--input=*patchfile*'

> Read the patch from *patchfile* rather than from standard input. See Section 15.1 [patch Options], page 69.

'-l'
'--ignore-white-space'

> Let any sequence of blanks (spaces or tabs) in the patch file match any sequence of blanks in the input file. See Section 10.3.1 [Changed White Space], page 46.

'-n'
'--normal'

> Interpret the patch file as a normal diff. See Section 10.1 [patch Input], page 45.

'-N'
'--forward'
>   Ignore patches that `patch` thinks are reversed or already applied. See also '-R'.
>   See Section 10.3.2 [Reversed Patches], page 46.

'--no-backup-if-mismatch'
>   Do not back up the original contents of files. This is the default behavior when
>   conforming to POSIX. See Section 10.8 [Backups], page 50.

'-o *file*'
'--output=*file*'
>   Use *file* as the output file name. See Section 15.1 [patch Options], page 69.

'-p*number*'
'--strip=*number*'
>   Set the file name strip count to *number*. See Section 10.7 [patch Directories],
>   page 49.

'--posix'   Conform to POSIX, as if the `POSIXLY_CORRECT` environment variable had been
>   set. See Section 10.12 [patch and POSIX], page 53.

'--quoting-style=*word*'
>   Use style *word* to quote names in diagnostics, as if the `QUOTING_STYLE` environ-
>   ment variable had been set to *word*. See Section 10.11.3 [patch Quoting Style],
>   page 52.

'-r *reject-file*'
'--reject-file=*reject-file*'
>   Use *reject-file* as the reject file name. See Section 10.10 [Reject Names], page 51.

'-R'
'--reverse'
>   Assume that this patch was created with the old and new files swapped. See
>   Section 10.3.2 [Reversed Patches], page 46.

'-s'
'--quiet'
'--silent'
>   Work silently unless an error occurs. See Section 10.11 [patch Messages],
>   page 51.

'-t'
'--batch'   Do not ask any questions. See Section 10.11 [patch Messages], page 51.

'-T'
'--set-time'
>   Set the modification and access times of patched files from time stamps given
>   in context diff headers, assuming that the context diff headers use local time.
>   See Section 10.5 [Patching Time Stamps], page 48.

'-u'
'--unified'
>   Interpret the patch file as a unified diff. See Section 10.1 [patch Input], page 45.

'-v'
'--version'
>   Output version information and then exit.

'-V *backup-style*'
'--version=control=*backup-style*'
>   Select the naming convention for backup file names. See Section 10.9 [Backup
>   Names], page 50.

'--verbose'
>   Print more diagnostics than usual. See Section 10.11 [patch Messages], page 51.

'-x *number*'
'--debug=*number*'
>   Set internal debugging flags. Of interest only to patch patchers.

'-Y *prefix*'
'--basename-prefix=*prefix*'
>   Prepend *prefix* to base names of backup files. See Section 10.9 [Backup Names],
>   page 50.

'-z *suffix*'
'--suffix=*suffix*'
>   Use *suffix* as the backup extension instead of '.orig' or '~'. See Section 10.9
>   [Backup Names], page 50.

'-Z'
'--set-utc'
>   Set the modification and access times of patched files from time stamps given
>   in context diff headers, assuming that the context diff headers use UTC. See
>   Section 10.5 [Patching Time Stamps], page 48.

16 Invoking `sdiff`

The `sdiff` command merges two files and interactively outputs the results. Its arguments are as follows:

    sdiff -o outfile options... from-file to-file

This merges *from-file* with *to-file*, with output to *outfile*. If *from-file* is a directory and *to-file* is not, `sdiff` compares the file in *from-file* whose file name is that of *to-file*, and vice versa. *from-file* and *to-file* may not both be directories.

`sdiff` options begin with '-', so normally *from-file* and *to-file* may not begin with '-'. However, '--' as an argument by itself treats the remaining arguments as file names even if they begin with '-'. You may not use '-' as an input file.

`sdiff` without '--output' ('-o') produces a side-by-side difference. This usage is obsolete; use the '--side-by-side' ('-y') option of `diff` instead.

An exit status of 0 means no differences were found, 1 means some differences were found, and 2 means trouble.

16.1 Options to `sdiff`

Below is a summary of all of the options that GNU `sdiff` accepts. Each option has two equivalent names, one of which is a single letter preceded by '-', and the other of which is a long name preceded by '--'. Multiple single letter options (unless they take an argument) can be combined into a single command line argument. Long named options can be abbreviated to any unique prefix of their name.

'-a'
'--text'   Treat all files as text and compare them line-by-line, even if they do not appear to be text. See Section 1.7 [Binary], page 6.

'-b'
'--ignore-space-change'
             Ignore changes in amount of white space. See Section 1.2 [White Space], page 4.

'-B'
'--ignore-blank-lines'
             Ignore changes that just insert or delete blank lines. See Section 1.3 [Blank Lines], page 4.

'-d'
'--minimal'
             Change the algorithm to perhaps find a smaller set of changes. This makes `sdiff` slower (sometimes much slower). See Chapter 6 [diff Performance], page 33.

'--diff-program=*program*'
             Use the compatible comparison program *program* to compare files instead of `diff`.

'-E'
'--ignore-tab-expansion'
             Ignore changes due to tab expansion. See Section 1.2 [White Space], page 4.

'--help'   Output a summary of usage and then exit.

'-i'
'--ignore-case'
        Ignore changes in case; consider upper- and lower-case to be the same. See
        Section 1.5 [Case Folding], page 5.

'-I *regexp*'
'--ignore-matching-lines=*regexp*'
        Ignore changes that just insert or delete lines that match *regexp*. See Section 1.4
        [Specified Lines], page 5.

'-l'
'--left-column'
        Print only the left column of two common lines. See Section 2.3.1 [Side by Side
        Format], page 15.

'-o *file*'
'--output=*file*'
        Put merged output into *file*. This option is required for merging.

'-s'
'--suppress-common-lines'
        Do not print common lines. See Section 2.3.1 [Side by Side Format], page 15.

'--speed-large-files'
        Use heuristics to speed handling of large files that have numerous scattered
        small changes. See Chapter 6 [diff Performance], page 33.

'--strip-trailing-cr'
        Strip any trailing carriage return at the end of an input line. See Section 1.7
        [Binary], page 6.

'-t'
'--expand-tabs'
        Expand tabs to spaces in the output, to preserve the alignment of tabs in the
        input files. See Section 5.1 [Tabs], page 31.

'--tabsize=*columns*'
        Assume that tab stops are set every *columns* (default 8) print columns. See
        Section 5.1 [Tabs], page 31.

'-v'
'--version'
        Output version information and then exit.

'-w *columns*'
'--width=*columns*'
        Output at most *columns* (default 130) print columns per line. See Section 2.3.1
        [Side by Side Format], page 15. Note that for historical reasons, this option is
        '-W' in diff, '-w' in sdiff.

'`-W`'
'`--ignore-all-space`'
> Ignore white space when comparing lines. See Section 1.2 [White Space], page 4.
> Note that for historical reasons, this option is '`-w`' in `diff`, '`-W`' in `sdiff`.

'`-Z`'
'`--ignore-trailing-space`'
> Ignore white space at line end. See Section 1.2 [White Space], page 4.

17 Standards conformance

In a few cases, the GNU utilities' default behavior is incompatible with the POSIX standard. To suppress these incompatibilities, define the `POSIXLY_CORRECT` environment variable. Unless you are checking for POSIX conformance, you probably do not need to define `POSIXLY_CORRECT`.

Normally options and operands can appear in any order, and programs act as if all the options appear before any operands. For example, 'diff lao tzu -C 2' acts like 'diff -C 2 lao tzu', since '2' is an option-argument of '-C'. However, if the `POSIXLY_CORRECT` environment variable is set, options must appear before operands, unless otherwise specified for a particular command.

Newer versions of POSIX are occasionally incompatible with older versions. For example, older versions of POSIX allowed the command 'diff -c -10' to have the same meaning as 'diff -C 10', but POSIX 1003.1-2001 'diff' no longer allows digit-string options like '-10'.

The GNU utilities normally conform to the version of POSIX that is standard for your system. To cause them to conform to a different version of POSIX, define the `_POSIX2_VERSION` environment variable to a value of the form *yyyymm* specifying the year and month the standard was adopted. Two values are currently supported for `_POSIX2_VERSION`: '199209' stands for POSIX 1003.2-1992, and '200112' stands for POSIX 1003.1-2001. For example, if you are running older software that assumes an older version of POSIX and uses 'diff -c -10', you can work around the compatibility problems by setting '_POSIX2_VERSION=199209' in your environment.

18 Future Projects

Here are some ideas for improving GNU `diff` and `patch`. The GNU project has identified some improvements as potential programming projects for volunteers. You can also help by reporting any bugs that you find.

If you are a programmer and would like to contribute something to the GNU project, please consider volunteering for one of these projects. If you are seriously contemplating work, please write to gvc@gnu.org to coordinate with other volunteers.

18.1 Suggested Projects for Improving GNU `diff` and `patch`

One should be able to use GNU `diff` to generate a patch from any pair of directory trees, and given the patch and a copy of one such tree, use `patch` to generate a faithful copy of the other. Unfortunately, some changes to directory trees cannot be expressed using current patch formats; also, `patch` does not handle some of the existing formats. These shortcomings motivate the following suggested projects.

18.1.1 Handling Multibyte and Varying-Width Characters

`diff`, `diff3` and `sdiff` treat each line of input as a string of unibyte characters. This can mishandle multibyte characters in some cases. For example, when asked to ignore spaces, `diff` does not properly ignore a multibyte space character.

Also, `diff` currently assumes that each byte is one column wide, and this assumption is incorrect in some locales, e.g., locales that use UTF-8 encoding. This causes problems with the '-y' or '--side-by-side' option of `diff`.

These problems need to be fixed without unduly affecting the performance of the utilities in unibyte environments.

The IBM GNU/Linux Technology Center Internationalization Team has proposed patches to support internationalized `diff`. Unfortunately, these patches are incomplete and are to an older version of `diff`, so more work needs to be done in this area.

18.1.2 Handling Changes to the Directory Structure

`diff` and `patch` do not handle some changes to directory structure. For example, suppose one directory tree contains a directory named 'D' with some subsidiary files, and another contains a file with the same name 'D'. 'diff -r' does not output enough information for `patch` to transform the directory subtree into the file.

There should be a way to specify that a file has been removed without having to include its entire contents in the patch file. There should also be a way to tell `patch` that a file was renamed, even if there is no way for `diff` to generate such information. There should be a way to tell `patch` that a file's time stamp has changed, even if its contents have not changed.

These problems can be fixed by extending the `diff` output format to represent changes in directory structure, and extending `patch` to understand these extensions.

18.1.3 Files that are Neither Directories Nor Regular Files

Some files are neither directories nor regular files: they are unusual files like symbolic links, device special files, named pipes, and sockets. Currently, `diff` treats symbolic links as if they were the pointed-to files, except that a recursive `diff` reports an error if it detects infinite loops of symbolic links (e.g., symbolic links to '..'). `diff` treats other special files like regular files if they are specified at the top level, but simply reports their presence when comparing directories. This means that `patch` cannot represent changes to such files. For example, if you change which file a symbolic link points to, `diff` outputs the difference between the two files, instead of the change to the symbolic link.

`diff` should optionally report changes to special files specially, and `patch` should be extended to understand these extensions.

18.1.4 File Names that Contain Unusual Characters

When a file name contains an unusual character like a newline or white space, 'diff -r' generates a patch that `patch` cannot parse. The problem is with format of `diff` output, not just with `patch`, because with odd enough file names one can cause `diff` to generate a patch that is syntactically correct but patches the wrong files. The format of `diff` output should be extended to handle all possible file names.

18.1.5 Outputting Diffs in Time Stamp Order

Applying `patch` to a multiple-file diff can result in files whose time stamps are out of order. GNU `patch` has options to restore the time stamps of the updated files (see Section 10.5 [Patching Time Stamps], page 48), but sometimes it is useful to generate a patch that works even if the recipient does not have GNU patch, or does not use these options. One way to do this would be to implement a `diff` option to output diffs in time stamp order.

18.1.6 Ignoring Certain Changes

It would be nice to have a feature for specifying two strings, one in *from-file* and one in *to-file*, which should be considered to match. Thus, if the two strings are 'foo' and 'bar', then if two lines differ only in that 'foo' in file 1 corresponds to 'bar' in file 2, the lines are treated as identical.

It is not clear how general this feature can or should be, or what syntax should be used for it.

A partial substitute is to filter one or both files before comparing, e.g.:

```
sed 's/foo/bar/g' file1 | diff - file2
```

However, this outputs the filtered text, not the original.

18.1.7 Improving Performance

When comparing two large directory structures, one of which was originally copied from the other with time stamps preserved (e.g., with 'cp -pR'), it would greatly improve performance if an option told `diff` to assume that two files with the same size and time stamps have the same content. See Chapter 6 [diff Performance], page 33.

18.2 Reporting Bugs

If you think you have found a bug in GNU `cmp`, `diff`, `diff3`, or `sdiff`, please report it by electronic mail to the GNU utilities bug report mailing list bug-gnu-utils@gnu.org. Please send bug reports for GNU `patch` to bug-patch@gnu.org. Send as precise a description of the problem as you can, including the output of the '--version' option and sample input files that produce the bug, if applicable. If you have a nontrivial fix for the bug, please send it as well. If you have a patch, please send it too. It may simplify the maintainer's job if the patch is relative to a recent test release, which you can find in the directory `ftp://alpha.gnu.org/gnu/diffutils/`.

Appendix A Copying This Manual

Version 1.3, 3 November 2008

Copyright © 2000, 2001, 2002, 2007, 2008 Free Software Foundation, Inc.
http://fsf.org/

Everyone is permitted to copy and distribute verbatim copies
of this license document, but changing it is not allowed.

0. PREAMBLE

The purpose of this License is to make a manual, textbook, or other functional and useful document *free* in the sense of freedom: to assure everyone the effective freedom to copy and redistribute it, with or without modifying it, either commercially or non-commercially. Secondarily, this License preserves for the author and publisher a way to get credit for their work, while not being considered responsible for modifications made by others.

This License is a kind of "copyleft", which means that derivative works of the document must themselves be free in the same sense. It complements the GNU General Public License, which is a copyleft license designed for free software.

We have designed this License in order to use it for manuals for free software, because free software needs free documentation: a free program should come with manuals providing the same freedoms that the software does. But this License is not limited to software manuals; it can be used for any textual work, regardless of subject matter or whether it is published as a printed book. We recommend this License principally for works whose purpose is instruction or reference.

1. APPLICABILITY AND DEFINITIONS

This License applies to any manual or other work, in any medium, that contains a notice placed by the copyright holder saying it can be distributed under the terms of this License. Such a notice grants a world-wide, royalty-free license, unlimited in duration, to use that work under the conditions stated herein. The "Document", below, refers to any such manual or work. Any member of the public is a licensee, and is addressed as "you". You accept the license if you copy, modify or distribute the work in a way requiring permission under copyright law.

A "Modified Version" of the Document means any work containing the Document or a portion of it, either copied verbatim, or with modifications and/or translated into another language.

A "Secondary Section" is a named appendix or a front-matter section of the Document that deals exclusively with the relationship of the publishers or authors of the Document to the Document's overall subject (or to related matters) and contains nothing that could fall directly within that overall subject. (Thus, if the Document is in part a textbook of mathematics, a Secondary Section may not explain any mathematics.) The relationship could be a matter of historical connection with the subject or with related matters, or of legal, commercial, philosophical, ethical or political position regarding them.

The "Invariant Sections" are certain Secondary Sections whose titles are designated, as being those of Invariant Sections, in the notice that says that the Document is released under this License. If a section does not fit the above definition of Secondary then it is not allowed to be designated as Invariant. The Document may contain zero Invariant Sections. If the Document does not identify any Invariant Sections then there are none.

The "Cover Texts" are certain short passages of text that are listed, as Front-Cover Texts or Back-Cover Texts, in the notice that says that the Document is released under this License. A Front-Cover Text may be at most 5 words, and a Back-Cover Text may be at most 25 words.

A "Transparent" copy of the Document means a machine-readable copy, represented in a format whose specification is available to the general public, that is suitable for revising the document straightforwardly with generic text editors or (for images composed of pixels) generic paint programs or (for drawings) some widely available drawing editor, and that is suitable for input to text formatters or for automatic translation to a variety of formats suitable for input to text formatters. A copy made in an otherwise Transparent file format whose markup, or absence of markup, has been arranged to thwart or discourage subsequent modification by readers is not Transparent. An image format is not Transparent if used for any substantial amount of text. A copy that is not "Transparent" is called "Opaque".

Examples of suitable formats for Transparent copies include plain ASCII without markup, Texinfo input format, LaTeX input format, SGML or XML using a publicly available DTD, and standard-conforming simple HTML, PostScript or PDF designed for human modification. Examples of transparent image formats include PNG, XCF and JPG. Opaque formats include proprietary formats that can be read and edited only by proprietary word processors, SGML or XML for which the DTD and/or processing tools are not generally available, and the machine-generated HTML, PostScript or PDF produced by some word processors for output purposes only.

The "Title Page" means, for a printed book, the title page itself, plus such following pages as are needed to hold, legibly, the material this License requires to appear in the title page. For works in formats which do not have any title page as such, "Title Page" means the text near the most prominent appearance of the work's title, preceding the beginning of the body of the text.

The "publisher" means any person or entity that distributes copies of the Document to the public.

A section "Entitled XYZ" means a named subunit of the Document whose title either is precisely XYZ or contains XYZ in parentheses following text that translates XYZ in another language. (Here XYZ stands for a specific section name mentioned below, such as "Acknowledgements", "Dedications", "Endorsements", or "History".) To "Preserve the Title" of such a section when you modify the Document means that it remains a section "Entitled XYZ" according to this definition.

The Document may include Warranty Disclaimers next to the notice which states that this License applies to the Document. These Warranty Disclaimers are considered to be included by reference in this License, but only as regards disclaiming warranties: any other implication that these Warranty Disclaimers may have is void and has no effect on the meaning of this License.

2. VERBATIM COPYING

You may copy and distribute the Document in any medium, either commercially or noncommercially, provided that this License, the copyright notices, and the license notice saying this License applies to the Document are reproduced in all copies, and that you add no other conditions whatsoever to those of this License. You may not use technical measures to obstruct or control the reading or further copying of the copies you make or distribute. However, you may accept compensation in exchange for copies. If you distribute a large enough number of copies you must also follow the conditions in section 3.

You may also lend copies, under the same conditions stated above, and you may publicly display copies.

3. COPYING IN QUANTITY

If you publish printed copies (or copies in media that commonly have printed covers) of the Document, numbering more than 100, and the Document's license notice requires Cover Texts, you must enclose the copies in covers that carry, clearly and legibly, all these Cover Texts: Front-Cover Texts on the front cover, and Back-Cover Texts on the back cover. Both covers must also clearly and legibly identify you as the publisher of these copies. The front cover must present the full title with all words of the title equally prominent and visible. You may add other material on the covers in addition. Copying with changes limited to the covers, as long as they preserve the title of the Document and satisfy these conditions, can be treated as verbatim copying in other respects.

If the required texts for either cover are too voluminous to fit legibly, you should put the first ones listed (as many as fit reasonably) on the actual cover, and continue the rest onto adjacent pages.

If you publish or distribute Opaque copies of the Document numbering more than 100, you must either include a machine-readable Transparent copy along with each Opaque copy, or state in or with each Opaque copy a computer-network location from which the general network-using public has access to download using public-standard network protocols a complete Transparent copy of the Document, free of added material. If you use the latter option, you must take reasonably prudent steps, when you begin distribution of Opaque copies in quantity, to ensure that this Transparent copy will remain thus accessible at the stated location until at least one year after the last time you distribute an Opaque copy (directly or through your agents or retailers) of that edition to the public.

It is requested, but not required, that you contact the authors of the Document well before redistributing any large number of copies, to give them a chance to provide you with an updated version of the Document.

4. MODIFICATIONS

You may copy and distribute a Modified Version of the Document under the conditions of sections 2 and 3 above, provided that you release the Modified Version under precisely this License, with the Modified Version filling the role of the Document, thus licensing distribution and modification of the Modified Version to whoever possesses a copy of it. In addition, you must do these things in the Modified Version:

A. Use in the Title Page (and on the covers, if any) a title distinct from that of the Document, and from those of previous versions (which should, if there were any, be listed in the History section of the Document). You may use the same title as a previous version if the original publisher of that version gives permission.

B. List on the Title Page, as authors, one or more persons or entities responsible for authorship of the modifications in the Modified Version, together with at least five of the principal authors of the Document (all of its principal authors, if it has fewer than five), unless they release you from this requirement.

C. State on the Title page the name of the publisher of the Modified Version, as the publisher.

D. Preserve all the copyright notices of the Document.

E. Add an appropriate copyright notice for your modifications adjacent to the other copyright notices.

F. Include, immediately after the copyright notices, a license notice giving the public permission to use the Modified Version under the terms of this License, in the form shown in the Addendum below.

G. Preserve in that license notice the full lists of Invariant Sections and required Cover Texts given in the Document's license notice.

H. Include an unaltered copy of this License.

I. Preserve the section Entitled "History", Preserve its Title, and add to it an item stating at least the title, year, new authors, and publisher of the Modified Version as given on the Title Page. If there is no section Entitled "History" in the Document, create one stating the title, year, authors, and publisher of the Document as given on its Title Page, then add an item describing the Modified Version as stated in the previous sentence.

J. Preserve the network location, if any, given in the Document for public access to a Transparent copy of the Document, and likewise the network locations given in the Document for previous versions it was based on. These may be placed in the "History" section. You may omit a network location for a work that was published at least four years before the Document itself, or if the original publisher of the version it refers to gives permission.

K. For any section Entitled "Acknowledgements" or "Dedications", Preserve the Title of the section, and preserve in the section all the substance and tone of each of the contributor acknowledgements and/or dedications given therein.

L. Preserve all the Invariant Sections of the Document, unaltered in their text and in their titles. Section numbers or the equivalent are not considered part of the section titles.

M. Delete any section Entitled "Endorsements". Such a section may not be included in the Modified Version.

N. Do not retitle any existing section to be Entitled "Endorsements" or to conflict in title with any Invariant Section.

O. Preserve any Warranty Disclaimers.

If the Modified Version includes new front-matter sections or appendices that qualify as Secondary Sections and contain no material copied from the Document, you may at your option designate some or all of these sections as invariant. To do this, add their titles to the list of Invariant Sections in the Modified Version's license notice. These titles must be distinct from any other section titles.

You may add a section Entitled "Endorsements", provided it contains nothing but endorsements of your Modified Version by various parties—for example, statements of peer review or that the text has been approved by an organization as the authoritative definition of a standard.

You may add a passage of up to five words as a Front-Cover Text, and a passage of up to 25 words as a Back-Cover Text, to the end of the list of Cover Texts in the Modified Version. Only one passage of Front-Cover Text and one of Back-Cover Text may be added by (or through arrangements made by) any one entity. If the Document already includes a cover text for the same cover, previously added by you or by arrangement made by the same entity you are acting on behalf of, you may not add another; but you may replace the old one, on explicit permission from the previous publisher that added the old one.

The author(s) and publisher(s) of the Document do not by this License give permission to use their names for publicity for or to assert or imply endorsement of any Modified Version.

5. COMBINING DOCUMENTS

You may combine the Document with other documents released under this License, under the terms defined in section 4 above for modified versions, provided that you include in the combination all of the Invariant Sections of all of the original documents, unmodified, and list them all as Invariant Sections of your combined work in its license notice, and that you preserve all their Warranty Disclaimers.

The combined work need only contain one copy of this License, and multiple identical Invariant Sections may be replaced with a single copy. If there are multiple Invariant Sections with the same name but different contents, make the title of each such section unique by adding at the end of it, in parentheses, the name of the original author or publisher of that section if known, or else a unique number. Make the same adjustment to the section titles in the list of Invariant Sections in the license notice of the combined work.

In the combination, you must combine any sections Entitled "History" in the various original documents, forming one section Entitled "History"; likewise combine any sections Entitled "Acknowledgements", and any sections Entitled "Dedications". You must delete all sections Entitled "Endorsements."

6. COLLECTIONS OF DOCUMENTS

You may make a collection consisting of the Document and other documents released under this License, and replace the individual copies of this License in the various documents with a single copy that is included in the collection, provided that you follow the rules of this License for verbatim copying of each of the documents in all other respects.

You may extract a single document from such a collection, and distribute it individually under this License, provided you insert a copy of this License into the extracted document, and follow this License in all other respects regarding verbatim copying of that document.

7. AGGREGATION WITH INDEPENDENT WORKS

A compilation of the Document or its derivatives with other separate and independent documents or works, in or on a volume of a storage or distribution medium, is called an "aggregate" if the copyright resulting from the compilation is not used to limit the legal rights of the compilation's users beyond what the individual works permit. When the Document is included in an aggregate, this License does not apply to the other works in the aggregate which are not themselves derivative works of the Document.

If the Cover Text requirement of section 3 is applicable to these copies of the Document, then if the Document is less than one half of the entire aggregate, the Document's Cover Texts may be placed on covers that bracket the Document within the aggregate, or the electronic equivalent of covers if the Document is in electronic form. Otherwise they must appear on printed covers that bracket the whole aggregate.

8. TRANSLATION

Translation is considered a kind of modification, so you may distribute translations of the Document under the terms of section 4. Replacing Invariant Sections with translations requires special permission from their copyright holders, but you may include translations of some or all Invariant Sections in addition to the original versions of these Invariant Sections. You may include a translation of this License, and all the license notices in the Document, and any Warranty Disclaimers, provided that you also include the original English version of this License and the original versions of those notices and disclaimers. In case of a disagreement between the translation and the original version of this License or a notice or disclaimer, the original version will prevail.

If a section in the Document is Entitled "Acknowledgements", "Dedications", or "History", the requirement (section 4) to Preserve its Title (section 1) will typically require changing the actual title.

9. TERMINATION

You may not copy, modify, sublicense, or distribute the Document except as expressly provided under this License. Any attempt otherwise to copy, modify, sublicense, or distribute it is void, and will automatically terminate your rights under this License.

However, if you cease all violation of this License, then your license from a particular copyright holder is reinstated (a) provisionally, unless and until the copyright holder explicitly and finally terminates your license, and (b) permanently, if the copyright holder fails to notify you of the violation by some reasonable means prior to 60 days after the cessation.

Moreover, your license from a particular copyright holder is reinstated permanently if the copyright holder notifies you of the violation by some reasonable means, this is the first time you have received notice of violation of this License (for any work) from that copyright holder, and you cure the violation prior to 30 days after your receipt of the notice.

Termination of your rights under this section does not terminate the licenses of parties who have received copies or rights from you under this License. If your rights have been terminated and not permanently reinstated, receipt of a copy of some or all of the same material does not give you any rights to use it.

10. FUTURE REVISIONS OF THIS LICENSE

The Free Software Foundation may publish new, revised versions of the GNU Free Documentation License from time to time. Such new versions will be similar in spirit to the present version, but may differ in detail to address new problems or concerns. See http://www.gnu.org/copyleft/.

Each version of the License is given a distinguishing version number. If the Document specifies that a particular numbered version of this License "or any later version" applies to it, you have the option of following the terms and conditions either of that specified version or of any later version that has been published (not as a draft) by the Free Software Foundation. If the Document does not specify a version number of this License, you may choose any version ever published (not as a draft) by the Free Software Foundation. If the Document specifies that a proxy can decide which future versions of this License can be used, that proxy's public statement of acceptance of a version permanently authorizes you to choose that version for the Document.

11. RELICENSING

"Massive Multiauthor Collaboration Site" (or "MMC Site") means any World Wide Web server that publishes copyrightable works and also provides prominent facilities for anybody to edit those works. A public wiki that anybody can edit is an example of such a server. A "Massive Multiauthor Collaboration" (or "MMC") contained in the site means any set of copyrightable works thus published on the MMC site.

"CC-BY-SA" means the Creative Commons Attribution-Share Alike 3.0 license published by Creative Commons Corporation, a not-for-profit corporation with a principal place of business in San Francisco, California, as well as future copyleft versions of that license published by that same organization.

"Incorporate" means to publish or republish a Document, in whole or in part, as part of another Document.

An MMC is "eligible for relicensing" if it is licensed under this License, and if all works that were first published under this License somewhere other than this MMC, and subsequently incorporated in whole or in part into the MMC, (1) had no cover texts or invariant sections, and (2) were thus incorporated prior to November 1, 2008.

The operator of an MMC Site may republish an MMC contained in the site under CC-BY-SA on the same site at any time before August 1, 2009, provided the MMC is eligible for relicensing.

ADDENDUM: How to use this License for your documents

To use this License in a document you have written, include a copy of the License in the document and put the following copyright and license notices just after the title page:

```
Copyright (C)  year  your name.
Permission is granted to copy, distribute and/or modify this document
under the terms of the GNU Free Documentation License, Version 1.3
or any later version published by the Free Software Foundation;
with no Invariant Sections, no Front-Cover Texts, and no Back-Cover
Texts.  A copy of the license is included in the section entitled ''GNU
Free Documentation License''.
```

If you have Invariant Sections, Front-Cover Texts and Back-Cover Texts, replace the "with...Texts." line with this:

```
with the Invariant Sections being list their titles, with
the Front-Cover Texts being list, and with the Back-Cover Texts
being list.
```

If you have Invariant Sections without Cover Texts, or some other combination of the three, merge those two alternatives to suit the situation.

If your document contains nontrivial examples of program code, we recommend releasing these examples in parallel under your choice of free software license, such as the GNU General Public License, to permit their use in free software.

Appendix B Translations of This Manual

Nishio Futoshi of the GNUjdoc project has prepared a Japanese translation of this manual.
Its most recent version can be found at `http://openlab.ring.gr.jp/gnujdoc/cvsweb/cvsweb.cgi/gnujdoc/`

Appendix C Index

www.ingramcontent.com/pod-product-compliance
Lightning Source LLC
LaVergne TN
LVHW060146070326
832902LV00018B/2972